PRAISE for STORY Dash

"David Hutchens has a unique ability to coach business leaders to tell effective stories whilst modeling great storytelling. *Story Dash* is a modern classic. I work with senior leaders in transforming organizations, and I will recommend it with no hesitation for engaging any business audience, anytime, anywhere."

—Dr. Yvonne Sum, APAC head of transformation,
leadership and culture, L'Oreal

"At PayPal, I work with product teams seeking to connect with customers. In David's story workshop, I experienced the impact of discovering our stories firsthand. This guide is perfect for me to use as a product discovery coach with my teams. I feel completely prepared!"

—Laura Ward, principal, design and research,
product discovery, PayPal

"We brought David Hutchens' Story Dashes to our teams all across the USA and Canada to build our culture around our values. We got a lot more! It has been amazing to see our leaders exercise their influence. In fact, this week I've been telling stories to smooth a transition process. It's been awesome and fun, and all of our employees have moved from an anxiety state to an excited state. We have found no faster way to unleash our culture than through our stories."

—Aaron Frazier, senior vice president of operations, VCA Canada

"As the leader of STORY, a global network of storytellers around the world, I get exposed to some of the best, most successful storytellers of our time. While members of our community have won Oscars, hit *New York Times* Bestseller lists, and more, there are few who truly grasp the power of story to shape organizational narrative. David Hutchens does, perhaps better than anyone else I know. This is exciting content that you can immediately put to work!"

—Harris III, founder and CEO, Istoria Collective

"*Story Dash* is a masterpiece in its simplicity, beauty, and moving stories. It is a master class in leadership, storytelling, and organizational change. This is not just a helpful book, it is fun to experience. And David lives what he writes! He has helped our social enterprise, Thistle Farms, hone our stories and our leadership to be a more loving and trauma-informed community."

—Becca Stevens, entrepreneur, founder and president, Thistle Farms

"In reading *Story Dash*, I am reminded of all the PowerPoint presentations and meetings that fell flat. As a Quality and Continuous Improvement leader, if only I could have that time back! David Hutchens has created a kind and amazing approach to help leaders connect with their audience. I've rarely seen a better example of empathy. You got me believing again, my friend!"

—Matt Keyser, quality & improvement leader,
Fortune 100 overnight shipping corporation

"This book is my Innovation Team's guide to identifying, crafting and testing the stories they need to connect to their audiences. With practical tips, easy-to-use tools, and guides, David makes storytelling accessible to all of us. I'll be getting a copy of *Story Dash* for every member of my team!"

—Cindi Perrine, innovation principal director,
global innovation studio lead, Accenture

"David Hutchens does not waste our time. This is his dash to story, getting us down to the business of stories, because business is practical. Learn about the 30% rule, and how to use frameworks like the Deck and the Canvas that organize us into a story mind. If story is the new urgency, as David argues, then this is the new must-have manual."

—Paul Costello, executive director, AmeriCorps Project CHANGE;
founder, New Story Leadership; Storywise.com

"With David's help, I've gone from boring to interesting; and better yet, *effective*! Having David's knowledge now available in book form is a gift to business leaders everywhere."

—Rob McMonagle, VP of talent development and acquisition,
Asbury Communities Senior Living

"In *Story Dash*, David Hutchens beautifully illustrates not only why storytelling is the most powerful communication tool we will ever have, but also how those of us who question our storytelling abilities can improve by following a few simple practices."

—Hal Cato, CEO, Thistle Farms

"In a world of increasing struggle for attention, the ability to tell sound, powerful stories is an imperative for success. David is a fantastic storytelling guide. Our foundation has found his work to be invaluable."

—James Pond, MA, president, Governor's Early Literacy Foundation, in partnership with Dolly Parton's Imagination Library

"I wish I had this book five years ago! My team was working to encourage dramatic improvements in population health, but we lost people in our complex slides and graphs. Alas, we struggled because we did not know how to unleash our message in the form of a story. I am pleased to have this powerful book now! In my new role as Executive Director I intend to share it with my researchers so they can encourage systems change in population health and beyond."

—Rebecca Niles, executive director, System Dynamics Society

"Our team was rich with stories to share, but we lacked an effective framework to communicate the meaning of our work. The Story Dash changed that! Our time with David has had a lasting impact on the health of our enterprise."

—Chris Province, CEO, Purpose & Performance Group Consulting

"David has facilitated Story Dashes with Goodwill senior level executives. During his workshops we laughed, we cried, and we eventually told better stories. It was amazing! Today, Goodwill senior leaders are telling the stories that engage their peers, teams and other leaders in their communities."

—Everett T. Shupe II, EdD, senior director, leadership and learning, Goodwill Industries International

the STORY Dash! process

Grab a croissant.

STORY MINING

Strategic selection
with the
Story Dash Cards
or Leadership Story Deck

Build for impact with the

STORY canvas

BREATHING LIFE via the Tell Test

Focus, refine, and bring it to life.

Activate

Create engagement and belief so people will act.

Great job!
Who's up
for lunch?

Also by David Hutchens

Outlearning the Wolves:
Surviving and Thriving in a Learning Organization

Shadows of the Neanderthal:
Illuminating the Beliefs That Limit Our Organizations

The Tip of the Iceberg:
Managing the Hidden Forces That Can Make or Break Your Organization

The Lemming Dilemma:
Living with Purpose, Leading with Vision

Listening to the Volcano:
Conversations That Open Our Minds to New Possibilities

A Slice of Trust

Circle of the 9 Muses:
A Storytelling Field Guide for Innovators and Meaning Makers

STORY — Dash!

Find, Develop, and Activate Your Most Valuable Business Stories ... In Just a Few Hours!

David Hutchens

Matt Holt Books
An Imprint of BenBella Books, Inc.
Dallas, TX

BenBella Books, Inc.
10440 N. Central Expressway
Suite 800
Dallas, TX 75231
benbellabooks.com
Send feedback to feedback@benbellabooks.com

BenBella is a federally registered trademark.
Matt Holt and logo are trademarks of BenBella Books.

Printed in the United States of America
10 9 8 7 6 5 4 3 2 1

Library of Congress Congress Control Number: 2021931460
ISBN 9781950665990 (print)
ISBN 9781953295446 (ebook)

Copyediting by Elizabeth Degenhard
Proofreading by Lisa Story
Text design and composition by David Hutchens
Cover illustration and design by David Hutchens
Printed by Versa Press

For Emory and Ollie,
who are finding their stories

CONTENTS

Chapter 1: Make me BELIEVE

"If we win, it will be because of *people* and not *our solution*."

This was how Jeanette began her introduction of me to her team in Boston last year, and it didn't go over well.

First, this was a team of eighteen brilliant technology professionals who were building the solution that they hoped would result in their winning a contract worth $250 million. And now Jeanette was telling them that if they won, it wouldn't be because of their solution. So that was awkward.

And then there was Jeanette's use of the word "if." Yeah, they picked up on that.

I watched the technology team squirm in their seats. They didn't like it. But they knew it was true.

I get this a lot. Many groups who bring me in to help them find stories don't do it because they love stories, or because it's the cool new thing.

Often they call because they have been losing. They can't break through the noise. They don't sound any different from their competitors. Their teams and markets aren't engaging or taking action. Their brilliant

1

innovations are met with a shrug. The louder they shout, the less their audiences seem to care.

This group was no different. They were well aware because they had been hearing it from their markets. "Listen, we already know what you're going to sell us," one customer had told them, "because your competitor was just in here yesterday, and we know your solution is going to be pretty similar to theirs.

"What we want to know is, what makes you different? Show us who you are. *Make us believe in you.*"

And this technology firm was confused by the question. *What does that mean, "show you who we are"? In the past, we always won on solution. And now that's not enough?* This talk of "belief" was like an alien language to these masters of C++ and JavaScript. I could see the dismay on their faces.

And now they were looking me over. They didn't want me there. A quarter billion dollars were on the line, the presentation was on Monday, and they had a long weekend ahead of them.

"So, this is David," Jeanette said to the team. "He is going to help us find our stories. David, I'll let you take it from here. Let me know if you need me."

And then Jeanette left me standing there. *She left me.* Wait. What?

"Hey, guys," I said. "So, um, let's get to work."

A different language

If we win, it will be because of people.

Show me who you are.

Make me believe.

For a lot of really smart leaders who are really good at what they do, these are tough ideas. Almost every leader I know struggles with getting people engaged in the work they care about most.

I coached a talented young programmer in Mumbai named Dharya. He confessed to me, "I got into this business because I love code. But it's like, everything I'm doing now is about people."

Right. Organizations are people, and this flash of the obvious has implications for leaders who are discovering that they're being called to show up in a different way. Systems with people in them are characterized by the messy element of *emotion* and, for the leader seeking influence, that requires a specific set of skills. I see leaders continually making the mistake of treating their organizations as if they are primarily rational systems. When the system is stuck, they think, *Oh, people aren't moving. They must need more data.*

So they show up with slides. Dear Lord, the slides. You know what I'm talking about. They look something like this.

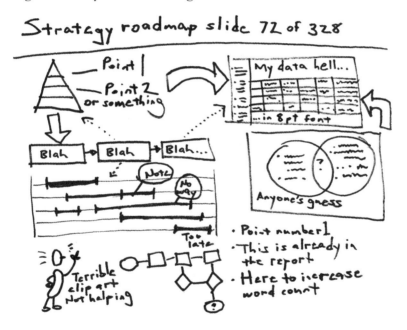

I was trying to be funny by exaggerating the slide, and I know I failed because the slides really do look like that. It's hard to overdo this stuff for comic effect. If I recall, the team in Boston was saying, "We could use a few more of those."

Data doesn't move people, especially in a world that has become infinitely noisy. In fact, attempts to influence people with data usually backfire and make people dig in their heels even more. The ways most leaders are attempting to unstick their systems are usually making them more stuck.

To lead in a new world of complexity, uncertainty, and ambiguity, twenty-first-century leaders are increasingly turning to one of humanity's oldest technologies. Story is the big, new idea that isn't new at all.

Organizations are emotional systems

"Organizations are emotional systems." I said that to a team of financial software engineers in Germany, and I was surprised that it was a controversial statement. I get it. These were brilliant people whose cool intelligence and data gymnastics had placed them near the top of their market. The idea that they might be finding their way through the world with emotion was an affront to some of them.

But they are. We all are. Our emotion drives our decision making. Our rationality shows up after the feeling, not before, adding justification to decisions that we've already made with our emotions.

Consider Elliot. Elliot was a rare exception to this rule. After a surgery to remove a brain tumor, he was left with permanent damage to the ventromedial prefrontal cortex area of his brain. As a result of the brain damage, Elliot's emotions became, in effect, walled off from his thoughts. He could still think thoughts. He could still feel feelings. But Elliot could no longer link the two.

The debilitating impact of this on Elliot's life is described in the book *Descartes' Error*[1] by Dr. Antonio Damasio, a neuroscientist who was also Elliot's doctor. Damasio shows that after the surgery Elliot could no longer hold down a job, finish a task, manage his finances, or keep a relationship.

In fact, unable to access to his emotion, even simple decisions had a paralyzing effect on Elliot. One day, Elliot was in Damasio's office when Damasio asked him when he wanted to schedule his next appointment.

1 Antonio R. Damasio, *Descartes' Error: Emotion, Reason, and the Human Brain* (New York, NY: G. P. Putnam's Sons, 1994).

"Would you like to come in next Monday morning, or Tuesday afternoon?" Dr. Damasio said.

He watched with fascination as Elliot stood there helplessly *for nearly half an hour,* lost in an endless loop of weighing pros and cons of Monday versus Tuesday, until Damasio finally intervened and said, "why don't we just grab that Monday date?" Elliot said "okay" and went on his way.

For most of us, the simplicity of that decision would belie a complicated and mostly invisible dance between our thoughts and our emotions. Your body draws from an archive of emotional memory that quickly assigns a felt value to the different choices. (Damasio calls these emotional memories "somatic markers.") We hardly notice this internal emotional transaction has taken place as we say things like, "You know, Tuesday feels good to me. Let's go with that."

Elliot couldn't do this. Unable to bring emotion into the equation, "Monday versus Tuesday" represented an endless maze of variables with no way of assigning weight or value to any of them.

You feel it first; thoughts follow. Your brain assigns language to justify a decision that was already made emotionally.

Sure, "Monday versus Tuesday" is a low-stakes decision. But emotion drives the most consequential activities of individuals, teams, institutions, and societies. The Boston team's client was pretty blunt that a complex, quarter-billion-dollar sales decision hinged on a feeling. *Make us believe.*

Organizations are emotional systems. If you are seeking to influence people to action by using data, you've grabbed the wrong tool from the toolbox. You need another language.

Story is the language that engages and influences the emotional system.

Make me believe

Stories aren't the answer to every challenge in leadership. But for moving the emotional system, there is no more potent lever.

When should you tell stories? Whenever you want to create *engagement and belief so that people will act.*

People who are engaged do something because they want to. The motive is coming from within them.

Belief is even more powerful. Believing something is a lot different from knowing something. You hold your beliefs much more deeply than your thoughts. Martyrs across history usually died for belief, not for data. And when one of the masters of this work, Steve Jobs, influenced his faithful believers to camp out in front of Apple stores for days awaiting the next iPhone, it wasn't because he told them the technical specs.

The Boston team needed the client to *know* how much their plan would cost and how long it would take. Fine. Put that data in the report for easy reference. But they needed the customer to *believe* that they could uniquely execute the plan with more resilience and creativity than any of their competitors.

For that, we found some stories to tell.

Today, leaders of all kinds are seeking to tell stories that create this powerful engagement and belief around the work they care about most. Imagine it: What if your teams, partners, and customers acted not because you pushed them, but because they believed in what you offered? What if they camped out on the sidewalk for you?

You should be telling your stories. You need a Story Dash.

Who is this book for?

I'll say it again: A Story Dash process is for anyone who needs to create engagement and belief so that people will act.

It's for scientists, technologists, and engineers who are working on brilliant innovations that are difficult to explain because they are so complicated that the rest of us don't understand it (much less get excited about it).

It's for innovators and leaders who must align people to act on a new idea or strategy, which is difficult because people would prefer for things to stay the way they are rather than step into the scary or untested unknown. Are you inviting the team into an innovation or design process? Build in some time for a Story Dash!

If you're selling something—and we all are—that's a no-brainer. Sales and marketing people have known this for a long time. I learned early in my career as an advertising copywriter in Atlanta that if I told a story, people would buy more Coca-Cola.

It's for product managers, who are competing for resources and mind-share within the organization. You're never going to launch if you can't first generate movement and support with your stakeholders.

It's for talent acquisition and talent management professionals who are competing to attract and keep the hot young talent. The new generation of young professionals have choices, and they are scrutinizing your culture and saying, "Show me who you are. Make me believe in you."

It's for individual leaders, entrepreneurs, self-employed professionals, artists, and job seekers who seek to establish their compelling, impossible-to-ignore voice in a crowded field. To build your own voice of leadership, there are some specific kinds of stories you should be telling about yourself.

If you work for a nonprofit, I bet you are already thinking about stories. There's no better way to ask for support in a crowded marketplace than by telling the "moments of impact" stories of the people you help. But there are some other, crucial stories that most nonprofit leaders forget to tell. In a Story Dash, you'll discover what they are.

Do you have young kids at home? Then this is for you, too. You have a window of opportunity to bring certain kinds of stories to the dinner table that will build safety, resilience, and growth in those fast-developing little hearts and minds.

Yes, a Story Dash will help you activate great stories that will create engagement, belief, and action in all the above applications.

Even better, the Story Dash process will help you do it *fast*.

Story is the new urgency

Everyone I know is moving fast, all the time, wading through an ever-rising tide of mind-numbing information. The team in Boston was only days away from one of the most business-critical presentations of their careers when they had the epiphany that they needed to create indelible moments of empathy if they had any hope of winning.

I worked with the senior team at a healthcare organization that was in the middle of the COVID-19 pandemic meltdown when they called me back. "Hey, remember that story-training program we canceled back in March so we could focus on surviving coronavirus? We've changed our minds. We need to tell our stories if we are going to keep ourselves afloat. And our CEO wants to be part of the process. He wants to know how fast we can do this."

The answer to that last question is "pretty fast."

For the past twenty years, I've been working with leaders in organizations all around the world in dozens of countries to help them find and tell their stories. Often, this takes place within an on-site or virtual learning experience called "The Storytelling Leader" that may be one or more days in length. This robust experience affords us the luxury of deeply exploring narrative as an organizational capability, with all of its implications for meaning making, culture creation, knowledge transfer, organizational development, branding and marketing, and more. It is a potent experience in bringing humanity to the organization and activating your own voice of leadership.

But the voices at the other end of the phone line are increasingly urgent. "We are falling behind. When can you get here? How fast can we do this?"

Story is the new urgency. The world is getting noisier, and engagement is an increasingly precious resource.

After testing with thousands of leaders from Silicon Valley innovators to French luxury brands to Asian life sciences and beyond, here's the promise I can now make with confidence: With the Story Dash process and the accompanying tools, you can find, develop, and begin to activate your most strategic and valuable stories (which I call "narrative assets") in about half a day.

Seriously. We've done this in four hours.

Actually, I've done it even faster. Because the Boston team was so crunched, I worked with their leaders individually in forty-five-minute mini-sessions to get their stories ready. It was a whirlwind I don't recommend, but they got it.

By the way—I know I've been keeping you in suspense about the Boston team; and I also know that one of the hallmarks of a good story is a satisfying conclusion. That, I can happily provide: They won that $250 million contract. Of course, the technical solution was brilliantly designed. And, they said that the stories were instrumental in creating the compelling, memorable, clarifying, and *human* connection that their client was seeking. (For those who ask me for an ROI on storytelling, I can point to at least one group who says it's worth $250 million.)

The Story Dash is an active and repeatable process that recognizes that you are in the middle of the work. You need to create action now.

This is personal

Despite the focus on immediacy, the Story Dash process also has long-lasting implications for your leadership journey. It is your "most human" language that is at the very heart of your influence. It feels powerful. I've had more than a few leaders tell me that the Story Dash experience was "profound." I bet that you, too, will experience the process awakening something deeply personal within you. It's bringing more of who you are to your leadership.

Last year, I brought this work to a group of inmates who were learning entrepreneurship at the Tennessee Prison for Women here in my home of Nashville. At the end of the program, one of the women told me, "I feel like I discovered another kind of intelligence that I didn't know I had." I haven't stopped thinking about that. It might be the best and truest feedback I've ever received. Yes. When you work with your stories, you will awaken a different kind of intelligence.

Have I mentioned that it's also a lot of fun? It is. It feels good. Once your team starts activating the stories, they will say, "Why haven't we been doing this?! We should bring this into more parts of our work."

You may even come to the same conclusion as Jeff Bezos, CEO of Amazon, who has institutionalized the capability at the highest levels of the organization. Bezos has famously outlawed PowerPoint slides in his meetings with senior leaders and demanded that they instead show up prepared to tell meaning-generating stories about the state of their businesses. "It's the smartest thing I ever did," Bezos said.

Once you start experiencing the astonishing power of narrative, you too will discover that this is a core structure that connects to the heart of organizational decision making, strategy, influence, organizational development, knowledge creation, and much more.[2] "Why haven't we been doing this?!"

In a few minutes, we will get you started with your first Story Dash. But first, there are a few issues I'd like to address. Because I know there are some things that you're worried about.

Can we talk about fear?

Almost everyone comes into this work with some reluctance. When I am in France or Germany, there's a certain look of suspicion: "So this emotional American has flown over here to make us tell stories?" They believe that American leaders are uniquely equipped for this, but I tell them that hasn't been my experience at all. Everyone, regardless of culture, shows up with some fear.

Yes, fear. You'll find that telling stories just feels more vulnerable, personally riskier, than data speak. Using language that is narrative has a way of opening you up so people can see more of who you are. It can be scary. That's why everyone would rather stay in data, and it's why so many

---

2 I have a book that can help you with those applications. See David Hutchens, *Circle of the 9 Muses: A Storytelling Field Guide for Innovators and Meaning Makers* (New York, NY: Wiley, 2015).

leaders over-rely on PowerPoint slides for their most mission-critical messages. Even when the stories you tell aren't particularly personal, there's
a noticeably "humanized" quality to the communication that some find
intimidating.

Let's just call out the fears, right here. I bet you have a few of these
self-defeating voices whispering in your head. Which of these have you
said to yourself?

"I'm not a storyteller."

This one is easy to address because it's the most demonstrably false. Yes,
you are a storyteller. If you had drinks or dinner with friends or family last
night, you told stories at the table, and then they jumped in and responded to your stories with more stories. You didn't even have to think about
it. Story is your brain's natural operating system for making sense of the
world. All we are doing is taking this most-human capability *that you already have* and connecting it more intentionally to the work that you care
about.

"I'm not a good public speaker."

You don't need to be. The Story Dash process is not about building your
public speaking skills. I've seen people tell stories while trembling with
nervousness, or struggling with English as a second language, and still
move the system to transformative action because they brought the right
story at the right time.

You may decide that building your presence as a speaker is indeed a
good next step in your development journey. That's a worthy investment
to make, but it's not the focus of the Story Dash. What this process *will*
deliver is high-impact stories that move people toward a strategic outcome
that you define.

"I don't want to sound like I'm performing."

Yeah, me neither. I hear this one a lot. No one wants to sound fake, or like an over-the-top actor, or like they are reciting a script. (One of my French leaders told me, *"Nous ne voulons pas ressembler à des Américains!»*) For many people the word "storytelling" implies a performance. But that's not what this work is about. It's using your authentic voice to talk about the work that matters most to you. You won't sound like you are performing. You will sound like *you.* Or to take it a step further, it will *unleash you.* It is a process of discovering and then amplifying your unique voice of leadership.

"I don't have any good stories." / "I can't think of any stories."

Hogwash. You are made of stories. Tonight when you go to sleep your brain will keep telling stories to you because *it can't stop.* Your problem is not that you don't have any stories; it's that you have *so many* that you don't know which ones to isolate and tell. The very next chapter will be revelatory for you.

"Listen, I get it. I'm a believer in story, but you have to understand— my boss/customer/partner is a data person or hard-driving personality and doesn't have any patience for this stuff."

The incorrect belief here is that "data people don't do story." But data is story. And story is data. (I heard one theorist explain that "story is data with a human soul.") As soon as you show me two data points on a financial chart and I ask, "Why did the line move from way up there to way down there?," your response will be story. Data requires sensemaking, and so story is always right there beneath the numbers.

12

Now, it might be true that your hard-driving, no-nonsense data boss or client doesn't have much patience for stories that are rambling or unfocused or irrelevant. They want you to get there fast and be on point. But you should still tell the story. Story Dash will help you with that.

"Stories take too long."

Not if you do it right. When you go to the movies, a story takes ninety minutes or more. But that's a different context because we go to the movies with an expectation of being entertained. We're telling stories not to entertain but to align, and in a context of leadership influence I have an appreciation for the elegantly constructed story. I find that many of the most powerful and persuasive stories can be told in about a minute or two. (In fact, there's a way to do this in as little as *five seconds*! Check out the "5-30-90 technique" on page 119.)

During your Story Dash you will encounter a cool resource called the Story Canvas that will help you articulate *why* you are telling your story. Once you have that clarity around outcome, you'll be amazed how much detail you *don't* need to get you there.

"I don't want to be all emotional; it's not my style."

I know some leaders who like to maintain a certain stoic presence. They don't want to become "all emotional" by telling a story that is, after all, a container for emotional content. But there's a difference between *displaying* emotion and *describing* it. I've seen leaders tell moving stories about the team's courageous or inspiring actions without ever changing their expressions, and it still creates powerful engagement. Again, this work is not about changing your voice or style. It's about amplifying it.

In summary, the tools, frameworks, and processes of a Story Dash have been designed to deliver strategic, persuasive, mission-focused stories that create powerful moments of connection with your audience, clarify the message, and close the deal. You'll amplify your authentic voice of leadership, while also creating engagement and belief that moves people to action around your mission-critical work. You'll do all of this by accessing an innate capability that you have long possessed. Folks, this one is a no-brainer.

In return, all the process asks is that you take a little risk. Show us who you are. Exercise your voice of leadership. Make us believe.

Setting the stage

A Story Dash is built on a unique suite of resources and frameworks that have been the product of nearly two decades of testing and experimentation.

Most of what you will need for the process is included with this book. There are a few additional items that can make your journey even richer. Before you begin, let's gather the materials you will need.

Story Dash Cards

There are six Story Dash Cards, available for download and printing at www.StorytellingLeader.com, which you can use to start identifying your story assets. You can also review the cards in Appendix 1 of this book. Go ahead and grab your copy now; you'll need them in the very next chapter.

Leadership Story Deck

The Leadership Story Deck is a full deck of cards, available separately, that contains dozens of additional ideas for stories that you can connect to your work, and which can also be used for a variety of team meaning-making activities. Leaders love this resource! It's like a little box of answers for leaders who aren't sure where to begin in their storytelling.

The cards in the Story Deck share the same design and purpose as the Story Dash Cards, but with dozens of cards you'll find that the collection is even more robust. The Story Deck will allow you to further position the Story Dash process to specific outcomes such as *innovation work, sales, strategy,* and more. (If you're interested in finding out more about the Leadership Story Deck, details are at www.StorytellingLeader.com.)

Don't have the Leadership Story Deck? That's not a problem. Simply download the six Story Dash Cards at www.StorytellingLeader.com. (Again, you can view them now in Appendix 1 at the back of this book.) The six cards will provide more than enough direction to get you started.

Story Canvas

The Story Canvas is a unique framework for visually developing your stories. It is a map that will prompt you to think through the elements of a story that create powerful engagement. Leaders who use the Story Canvas to develop their stories find that their messages land with much more impact as a result. A small version of the Story Canvas is presented in Chapter 3 of this book, and you are welcome to photocopy it. But this resource works best if you can print large copies so that every team member has their own. (In the United States, this will be on 11 × 17–inch "tabloid"-sized paper; in Europe and Asia, you will use A3 paper.) You can download the large Story Canvas in PDF format for free from www.StorytellingLeader.com.

Other resources

You'll need pens. Get some yellow Post-it®–style sticky notes. The classic square shape is ideal because they fit the Story Canvas.

Have some coffee, healthy snacks, or food around. Your brain is going to work hard and burn some glucose, and we want to keep the body energy balanced.

Oh, yes—get your team members! Yes, you can do this process individually. But as a team activity, it is a rich experience of shared meaning making that will create powerful connection and alignment. Note that

Appendix 3 contains facilitation notes that will aid a facilitator in managing the process for groups.

You can certainly do this work at your windowless conference room table. If you have something more relaxed—say, a flexible innovation space, or an offsite facility bathed in natural light and good energy—that's even better. Inviting a spirit of relaxed experimentation, trust, playfulness, and focused introspection serves this process well.

That's the setup. See? I told you this would be fast.

This book is meant to be experienced

One last thing: This book is meant to be experienced. I am inviting you into a process. It is active. Your learning depends on you actually working through the exercises so that you have experiential knowledge of a Story Dash.

If you read this book and then only think about it, you will miss the richness and nuance that can only be discovered by working through the steps. I suggest going through the process alone at least once. Then you'll have a base of experience that will help you lead your teams through the process.

Deal? Good.

Ready to tell some stories?

On your mark …

Get set …

the STORY Dash! process

Grab a croissant.

STORY MINING

Strategic selection with the
Story Dash Cards
or Leadership Story Deck

Build for impact with the

STORY canvas

BREATHING LIFE

via the Tell Test

Focus, refine, and bring it to life.

Activate

Create engagement and belief so people will act.

Great job!
Who's up
for lunch?

Chapter 2: Discover Your Narrative Assets with STORY MINING

Like many smart people I know, Steve Denning had an urgent message that no one seemed to care about.

This was in the 1990s, when Steve was a manager with the World Bank. He was an early advocate for a new organizational capability called *knowledge management*. He had a vision for the World Bank's leadership in knowledge management and he went around the world delivering a presentation to engage people in the vision, but he just couldn't drum up any enthusiasm for this new capability. Denning said people found the new idea "strange and generally incomprehensible."

One day, Denning changed the approach of his presentation. Instead of starting with the same old data that he always shared, he began with a story. This is the story he told (as recounted in his book *The Springboard: How Storytelling Ignites Action in Knowledge-Era Organizations*):

In June of last year, a health worker in a tiny town in Zambia went to the website of the Centers for Disease Control and got an answer to a question about the treatment of malaria. Remember that this was in Zambia, one of the poorest countries in the world. But the most striking thing about this picture, at least for us, is that our company, World Bank, isn't in it! Despite our know-how on all kinds of poverty-related issues, that knowledge isn't available to the millions of people who could use it. Imagine if it were. Think what an organization we could become.[1]

That was it. Short and simple. It takes less than a minute to tell.

It was a spark to a powder keg. People responded: "You mean we don't we have this capability at World Bank?! Why not? What's the holdup?" Suddenly, the incomprehensible idea was the hot idea. The Zambia story was the springboard that "unstuck" the system and engaged people on a transformative change journey. Today, the World Bank is a global leader in the modern knowledge management movement.

Denning says "the Zambia story" made it possible.

This almost seems too good to be true, doesn't it? "You mean all I have to do is tell a story and I can move the entire system?!"

I've seen it happen. Engaging the emotional system by using narrative language can truly have dramatic impacts.

But it's not a dog whistle. There's a lot that goes into it. It has to be done with skill, strategic intent, alignment with other organizational efforts, and consistency.

And you have to have the right stories. It starts with selection.

This is harder than it looks. After the fact, the Zambia story sounds perfect. *Of course* Steve should tell the Zambia story! It just works. It flows so clearly and naturally it almost seems obvious, doesn't it? It's not. You have to work backward, starting with clarity around your desired outcome. For Denning, it was: "I want people to believe that the emerging capability of knowledge management is critical to our future, that we are currently missing out, and that we should invest in it now."

Achieving that clarity is hard enough, but the next part is even

---

1 Stephen Denning, *The Springboard: How Storytelling Ignites Action in Knowledge-Era Organizations* (Oxford, UK: Butterworth-Heinemann, 2000).

harder: "What is a compelling story that will breathe life and urgency into this idea?" This is the part where people get stuck.

Try this for yourself. Reflect for a moment:

- What is the area of your work or leadership where you need to influence the "emotional system" to create engagement and belief? What action do you hope to move people to take?
- Now, consider: What are some stories that will engage people to take action around that outcome?

Feeling stuck?

Don't worry—this is the first point of intervention that the Story Dash process has been designed to help.

Let's do some *Story Mining*.

Here's how Story Mining works

Story work is like searching for gold. To find the valuable stories, you need to pan a lot of streams. In this metaphor, the "streams" are your (and your teammates') thoughts—a constant, fluid flow of human experiences, encoded in the deep, neural network of your minds as stories.

In some ways, it's a numbers game. We want to find a *lot* of stories. As you start surfacing stories, many of them will be "pretty good." But a few of them will be like Denning's Zambia story: so compelling, and so perfectly suited to your goals that you will find yourself telling them over and over again because you love the results they deliver. I call these value-holding stories *narrative assets*, and when you find one it's like uncovering a big nugget of shimmering gold.

We are mining for those narrative assets. To do this, you will use a series of story cards (either the Story Dash Cards available at www .StorytellingLeader.com, or the Leadership Story Deck) to increase your chances of isolating the stories most relevant to your work.

It's a fun process. Broadly, here's how it works.

First you will select specific cards that are most relevant to the goals you want to achieve.

The cards will prompt you to think of specific stories: "Oh, this reminds me of that time when…" You'll give each one a short title and capture it on a sticky note.

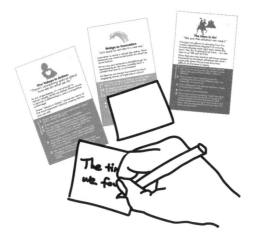

The goal at this stage of the process is quantity, not quality. We will develop them into great stories later. For now, we are trying to collect a lot of stories you didn't know you knew.

That's the broad process. Simple enough, right? Now let's hit the Deck and start uncovering some of your narrative assets.

Finding your Zambia

Everyone else in the group had their head down, scribbling story ideas on sticky notes. But Elizabeth was staring out the window with a glazed look in her eyes. I walked over, kneeled, and said, "Hey, Elizabeth. What's going on?" I knew exactly what her next words were going to be.

"I can't think of any stories," she said.

Yep. Knew it.

The irony was, I knew Elizabeth probably had the best stories in the room. Elizabeth was the head of a project team at a global consumer products company in Paris. Her project team was charged with reducing the materials used in product packaging and improving the company's environmental footprint. What a cool project! But her team had been stuck. Tasked with leading the change, they just had not been internally generating any energy or engagement around the project.

And now Elizabeth says she can't think of any stories.

This is not a failing on Elizabeth's part. Everyone struggles with this. Because we aren't typically directed to "try to think of a story about topic

X" (although that's a request I make all the time), it can feel unnatural. I still struggle with it, and I've been doing this for a few years.

This is why the Story Dash begins with strategic selection. *Which* stories should you be telling? How can we begin filtering our experiences and memories so they can be linked to a value-creating outcome? Answering this question has been the focus of much of my work.

After seeing so many leaders struggle, I began looking for ways to make it easier to identify stories. At the same time, as I heard leaders around the world tell thousands of stories, I began noticing some patterns. The same kinds of stories kept coming up, over and over again, depending on the context.

For example, when I worked with *sales and marketing* teams, I noticed that there were certain kinds of stories that salespeople kept telling.

Or in *innovation* work, there were different patterns of stories that seemed to be especially potent in that environment.

There were yet other stories that were unique to contexts of *culture and identity, knowledge transfer, strategy work,* and more.

I have even identified specific story types that are uniquely suited for building your *individual voice as a leader* or *your personal brand as an entrepreneur.*

I made notes of these patterns, and over the years I started curating these stories and grouping them into taxonomies of organizational story types. I started printing them up as little cards to trigger ideas for my clients so they could discover their own stories, and the response to the Leadership Story Deck was immediate: People loved having a little box of answers that was like a secret shortcut to finding their stories.

A closer look at the cards

Have the six Story Dash Cards next to you. (If you don't have them yet, you can view them in Appendix 1.) If you have the full set of Leadership Story Deck cards, remove the cover from the box, set the first six cards aside for now, and find the numbered cards that look like the image on the next page.

At the heart of the Story Mining process are a series of cards that capture stories that you could be telling about the work.

There are six Story Dash Cards, and there are a total of thirty-two cards in the Leadership Story Deck. They are similarly formatted.

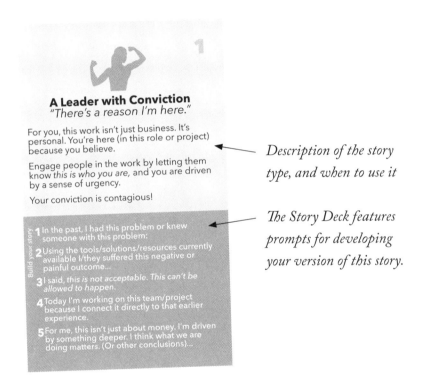

Description of the story type, and when to use it

The Story Deck features prompts for developing your version of this story.

Each has a description of the story type and when to use it at the top. This is the first card from the Leadership Story Deck, and you can see it's called "A Leader with Conviction: *There's a reason I'm here.*"

In the Story Deck, the bottom half of each card features a series of prompts that will help you develop your version of that story. The six Story Dash Cards are formatted a little differently; they each have a single prompt question to initiate your reflection about that story.

The back of each card has an example of what it sounds like when someone tells that story. These are all true stories that I have heard leaders tell. (I have changed names and other details to protect confidentiality.)

Flip the card over for an example of someone telling that story.

These examples on the back have a powerful utility. Often, when people are slowly sorting through the cards one at a time, they will find themselves stopping on one and thinking, *Oh, this story type is perfect for what I'm trying to accomplish. But I can't think of any stories like that.* If you find yourself thinking that, then flip the card over and read the example.

In the previous chapter, we talked about how telling stories at the dinner table will prompt other people to jump in and say, "Ooh, I have a story like that!" That's because a story activates the story network in your brain. Simply hearing someone tell a story will increase your odds of saying, "Ohhhh … wait a minute. That reminds me of that time when …" and *voilà*! Your brain just retrieved a story when you thought you didn't have one. Go ahead and give it a try. You'll find that you're more likely to pull a story from your memory.

About the six Story Dash Cards

If you don't have a copy of the Leadership Story Deck, that's not a problem. The six Story Dash Cards (which you can get at www.StorytellingLeader .com or view in Appendix 1) have been selected to address many of your leadership challenges. These six stories will take you far.

I curated these six cards based on a theory of organizational development called *appreciative inquiry* (AI). This is a powerful approach to organizational change that is driven by stories. It's built on a compelling idea: that organizational systems will naturally grow in the direction of the positive images and stories that we continually place in front of them. One of the founders of AI, Dr. David Cooperrider, says all organizational systems have three fundamental needs that leaders must attend to. The three needs are for *continuity, novelty,* and *transition.*[2]

These are foundational to your leadership. After all, as a leader your role is to point to the future and say, every day, in big ways and small ways, *we're going this way; follow me.*[3] You're constantly asking people to change, which people generally don't want to do. When you tell stories, you engage the emotional system and speed the path toward that change.

Let's take a look at these stories of *continuity, novelty,* and *transition* that are so powerful for your work.

Continuity stories

These stories are about core principles, values, and identity, which are the parts of your world that change very slowly. Most of the time, leaders of change should minimize disruption in these areas. People don't like it when you mess with "who we are." Even as you lead people to a bold future, you need to reassure them that "there are some things you can count on to remain the same." Of the six Story Dash Cards, the first two types speak to continuity. Perhaps you can quickly begin to intuit how these might connect to the work you are doing now:

 It Was True at the Beginning ("There's something special about how we began.")

 The Power of Our Values ("We won't compromise what makes us special.")

---

2 David L. Cooperrider, *The Appreciative Inquiry Handbook: For Leaders of Change* (San Francisco: Berrett-Koehler Publishers, 2008).

3 You might have noticed that the framework is, itself, a narrative: "We used to be back there, now we are going over there, and here are some things that are going to happen along the way." Story is fractal. We inhabit stories within larger stories.

Novelty stories

This is "the new." Here you are managing curiosity and how people dream. This *is* a place for stirring things up and challenging the way we do things. When you tell these stories, you say, "I want to show you what could be possible. Imagine if the world looked like *this* …" These future-focused stories are at the very heart of your leadership and innovation work. (Note that the Zambia story falls into this category.) The two cards that will help you surface your novelty stories are:

 Imagine If We Had That Here ("A possibility with power.")

Us at Our Best ("Imagine if more people did that!")

Transition stories

This is the journey. Here you are managing the shared story and the progress we are making as we move toward the future we desire. Your transition stories reveal what it looks like when we are solving hard problems, showing resilience, recovering from mistakes, and learning. These are the "how" stories, and I find that leaders consistently miss opportunities to tell these. You should be telling these stories to your customers! Let them peek behind the curtain and see what it looks like when the team is solving tough problems. ("Show me who you are!") The two transition-story cards are:

 One Courageous Personal Step ("We can overcome barriers with behaviors.")

 Eureka! ("What it looks like when we solve tough problems.")

Let's find your stories

Our first step is to select a few cards that you will use for your Story Mining. Four or five cards will work well.

There are a few ways to make these selections.

Review every card

If you wish, you can simply review the cards, one at a time. If you are using the six Story Dash Cards, you can do this quickly. If you're using the
twenty-seven cards in the Leadership Story Deck, allow yourself a few
more minutes.

As you review each story type, ask yourself, *Would a story like this support the work I'm doing?* (If you think *maybe* or *I'm not sure yet*, then that
card is a keeper for now.) Sort them into "keep" and "discard" piles until
you have narrowed it down to just a few.

If you are using the six Story Dash Cards from this book, you may
wish to use all six of them. Or there may be one or two that you discard
because they don't feel as urgent for your current needs.

Use the "Build Your Message" cards to focus your choices

The Leadership Story Deck has some special cards that will help you narrow down your choices. They are the black "Build Your Message" cards that
look like this:

These double-sided cards suggest possible stories that are ideally suited to different challenges, such as:

- Selling something, or creating a brand
- Aligning people around a strategy or a new possibility
- Developing a culture or building the team's identity
- Enabling innovation
- Sharing knowledge or fostering a learning organization
- Building your own voice as a leader or brand as an entrepreneur

Select the "Build Your Message" card that is closest to the challenge that you are working on.

Each "Build Your Message" card offers suggestions for four stories in the Deck that work especially well for that purpose. Pull those cards from the Deck and review. You'll see that the bottoms of the cards show an additional five or six ideas that could also work. Review those too.

When Elizabeth did her Story Dash, she had the Leadership Story Deck and was immediately drawn to the "Build Your Message" card that read *Align people to a strategy or new possibility.* That was clearly the best match for her project around packaging waste reduction.

She liked the suggestions on that card but also found a few others by flipping through the rest of the Deck. She also had the six Story Dash Cards, and so she reviewed those too. Ultimately, she decided that these five story types (three from the Leadership Story Deck and two from the Story Dash Cards) might be helpful for her purpose of engaging her organization around the packaging waste reduction project.

She then placed them in this sequence, because the stories build on one another to create a powerful message:

- "A Leader with Conviction" to show why she is personally motivated to lead the project.
- "Our Values in Action" to make the case that reducing packaging waste was, in fact, an expression of this company's most cherished beliefs.
- "Imagine If We Had That Here" to help her organization imagine (and then desire!) the outcomes that were possible.
- "Moments of Impact" to show that some of the early efforts at package waste reduction are, in fact, already delivering results and to encourage the organization to do more.
- "One Courageous Personal Step" to illustrate the kinds of small changes in behavior and attitude that people in the organization will need to make for the work to succeed.

That's already starting to sound like a powerful presentation!

Now it's your turn. Select your cards now.

Identify your stories

This is the fun part.

If you are doing this exercise as a team, I recommend each team member work individually so that you can compare your differing story ideas at the end of the exercise. You'll be amazed at the stories they have that you've never heard.

Spend about seven to ten minutes quietly reflecting on the cards you selected, one at a time.

Review the description on the front. Ask yourself, *When was a time when I (or someone I know) experienced something like that?*

If you are stuck and can't think of a story, read the example on the back and see if that helps to trigger a story idea.

If you continue to feel stuck, it is very possible that you are too fixated on finding "important" stories or "epic" stories. I see this happen all the time. The story might be a small moment! It may be a single conversation that happened over the phone, or something a team member did in a meeting. As you'll soon see, these small moments can have huge implications for your objectives. Later, we will make this "little" story into something compelling.

As you think of a story, simply give it a short title and write the title on a sticky note. There should be one story title per note.

Important: At this point, do not worry about how you will tell that story. That step will come later. For now, just get the idea written down—even if it is half-baked and not fully formed, and even if you are not yet "sold" that this is the ideal story.

Go for quantity. Get as many story ideas as you can.

You will likely experience clusters of ideas. That is, for some cards you may generate several ideas, while other cards may leave you "stuck" without a single sticky note.

That's okay. Again, we're going for overall quantity and aren't worried about achieving an even distribution of ideas.

When you are done, your work might look something like this:

The Story Mining process

1. Select four or five cards with story types that you think are relevant to your project, and fan out the selected cards in front of you.

2. Work individually. Allow seven to ten minutes for quiet reflection.

3. Review each story card. Ask yourself, *When was a time that I (or someone I know) experienced that?*

4. Trust the "small" story! Don't fall into the "epic importance" trap.

5. When you think of a story, give it a title. The title doesn't have to be creative, just something specific enough so that you can identify the story. Write the title on a sticky note and keep it next to the card.

6. Go for quantity. Get multiple story ideas.

7. Do not try to create the stories yet.

8. If working as a team, wait until everyone is done. Then compare your story ideas with one another.

Now reflect

How did that go? Was this exercise difficult?

Some people don't have any trouble identifying a large number of stories, while others struggle to think of just one or two. For some people, it is a new skill to sort through their memories and experiences for the purpose of capturing them and presenting to an audience. It can feel awkward and stiff at first, like exercising a muscle that you don't normally use.

Did you experience the "epic importance" trap in which you had a hard time trusting the smaller-scale stories? This may be an issue of confidence: "I just can't believe anyone will be interested in hearing me talk about this." That's fear raising its head again. Later when we build the story, you'll be amazed how powerfully those small-moment stories can move people toward the outcomes you want.

Over time, as you view your world through a "story lens" this will start to become more and more natural. The muscle will get stronger. You will start to notice value-creating stories happening all around you. And increasingly you will find yourself looking at team interactions and customer experiences, thinking in the moment, *That's a really great story! I should tell it to someone later! I know a team that needs to hear about that …"*

Congratulations on gathering lots of potential story assets! See? I told you that you had stories!

As you scan your cards and sticky notes you might even begin to sense—like Elizabeth did—a natural sequence for some of the stories you identified, and how they might be brought together for a powerful presentation. Hold that thought for now; we'll come back to it in Chapter 5.

As we continue moving quickly through our Story Dash, now may be a good time to refill your coffee and grab a snack. We are about to roll up our sleeves and bring your story ideas to life.

Epilogue: Nicolas at the beach

A few months ago I was working in a coffee shop when I received a message on LinkedIn from Elizabeth. Yes, I-can't-think-of-any-stories Elizabeth. The subject line of her message said "Follow up."

Her message was short: "Hello David, you may remember I was a participant in your storytelling program outside of Paris last year. I wanted to let you know the stories have changed everything. I always start now with the story of Nicolas at the beach. (Do you remember?) When I tell it, everyone listens. It is like casting a spell. Thank you for a great program."

Oh yes, I remembered "Nicolas at the beach."

It was prompted by the first card in the Leadership Story Deck: "A Leader with Conviction," which is one of the more powerful and flexible stories in the Deck. It was Elizabeth's "Why I'm Here" story that connected her personally to the packaging waste reduction project. The idea is, when you tell a "Why I'm Here" story, people are able to see your belief. Belief is socially transferable, and it becomes the audience's belief.

Amazingly, when we were all together in the program, Elizabeth was reluctant to tell her story at first.

Here's how it went:

Last summer, I was with my family at Plage le Bosquet in Portiragnes. It's one of our favorite beaches in the South of France.

And my eight-year-old son Nicolas came running up to me and my husband. He was wet from playing in the surf, and we said, *"qu'est-ce que c'est?"* He was holding a piece of plastic that had washed up on the shore. It was the plastic case for (one of our company's products). It was covered in seaweed but I could see our company logo. And, I will always remember the look in Nicolas's eyes when he said, "If this one washed up on the shore, I wonder how many more are in the ocean?" I could feel Nicolas' disappointment, and I felt like (our company) was a villain. So, for me, working on reducing waste in our packaging isn't just "business." It's personal. I will not forget the look on Nicolas's face. I won't stop working on this project until I am confident about the world I leave to him.

It was one of those stories that brought the room to a standstill.

I remember Elizabeth's self-critique: "This story is too much, *non*? It is very personal."

Everyone immediately assured her: "What?! No! That was amazing. You have to tell that story as part of this work!"

At the time, I could see that Elizabeth was not yet convinced. I recall she was concerned that the use of the word "villain" might be too pointed, but her team thought it might be the attention-getter they needed and that they should test it.

I was so glad to hear she had changed her mind and found her courage to tell the story that "cast a spell"—not just because of the implications for her own leadership and the success of the project, but for our shared future … and also for millions of kids like Nicolas.

Chapter 3:

Build for Impact with the

STORY canvas

I can tell Hema is nervous. In front of this audience, I might be too. She is telling her story to a senior group of managing partners, mostly men, who have flown in from across Asia, Europe, and the United States. There's a bit of a tremble in her voice, and she is holding her arms tightly crossed, almost in a self-protecting posture. But her words are electrifying.

Everyone in this audience knows about the SARS outbreak in India a few years earlier and its impact on their manufacturing facility in Bangalore. They had seen the dire numbers on the balance sheet. They knew how much it cost the company in financial terms.

But they've never heard this side of the story. Not like this.

Hema is telling the leadership team about the human cost of the crisis response to her team in Bangalore. When they closed the manufacturing plant, the local team experienced fear and threats from the surrounding community. They were shamed and ostracized. They quarantined themselves within the plant, away from their families, and put their lives on the line to prevent the facility from failing.

Hema's voice is barely above a whisper, and everyone in the room is holding their breath and leaning forward for this display of commitment and dignity. I see one leader subtly wipe his eyes, hoping that no one noticed.

After, I asked Hema how she was doing. "My heart is still beating fast," she confessed, but her wide smile told me that she was proud of how she exercised her voice of leadership. She knew that something significant had happened in the room.

In fact, everyone knew it. They felt it. They wanted to talk about the phenomenon afterward. "I could feel a moment when something shifted," one of the leaders said, and others nodded.

That impact extended beyond the event. I had a feeling the story would find its way across the organization, and it did. People talked. Hema's story was the beginning of a new, heightened support for the India team. Ultimately it resulted in the company making new investment in the Bangalore facility.

It is one of the story experiences that stands out for me because I can remember so well what it felt like in the room. Have you ever had that experience, in which you have been so drawn in by someone's story that you felt somehow transported? Neuroscience says this phenomenon is called *neural coupling*.

You can see neural coupling in brain scans. If I were to take an EEG of Hema's brain while she was telling her story, we would see her brain lit up with neural activity.

But here's the fascinating part: If I were to then scan the brains of an audience listening to Hema's story, we would see their brains lit up in a nearly identical pattern. Their brains, in a sense, changed shape to become like Hema's brain. They were linked together in a powerful moment of human connection.

Data doesn't create that connection. Your PowerPoint slides, no matter how good they are, will never create that connection.

Stories with emotional content create this neural coupling connection.

My colleague in this work, Michael McRay, likes to remind me of the old quote that "the shortest distance between two people is a story." That moment of powerful human connection is what we are chasing. That's the prize. And all of this work comes down to that simple idea: We want to bring that powerful "neural coupling" connection to more parts of the important work you do.

Hema's experience was no accident. It was intentional. She had planned for it in our Story Dash the day before. Hema had made some intentional choices about how to bring her personal experiences to this tough audience for a specific outcome. Her telling of the story was a strategic act.

You may have noticed I've been doing the same thing in this book, starting from the first page with the Boston technology team story. I am selecting certain stories to generate specific outcomes as I engage you in the Story Dash conversation. (In Appendix 4, I reveal how I am selecting and positioning these stories to engage you in specific ways.)

That's the goal of the next part of our Story Dash. In the Story Mining exercise, you identified some potential stories that might create engagement around your work. Now we want to develop those ideas into great stories that create that moment of connection. Every time.

To do this, we will need to turn our attention to the structure of stories. The path to the neural coupling connection is no mystery. We know what the elements are that create that connection. And once you know them, you can put them in your stories so that you can capture your audience too.

None of what I am describing here is new, by the way. I didn't invent any of this. People have been talking about the elements of story for a long time. Aristotle started cracking the code on story structure with *The Art of Rhetoric*, and that was in the fourth century BCE. These are all very old ideas that are now finding new application in modern innovation environments.

So, what are the story elements that generate neural coupling connection? You'll find them on the Story Canvas.

I will tell about the time I (or we)...

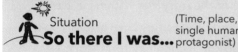

Situation (Time, place, single human protagonist)
So there I was...

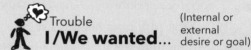

Trouble (Internal or external desire or goal)
I /We wanted...

But... (Lack of resources, external forces, limiting beliefs...)

Emotional data / somatic memory
I/we Felt...

Mad
frustrated annoyed
defensive
disgusted
outraged
offended

Sad
depressed
disappointed
regretful dismayed
disillusioned pessimistic
mournful

Happy
glad overjoyed
relieved
elated
pleased excited
grateful thrilled
content
amused
triumphant

Afraid
anxious
stressed vulnerable
nervous cautious
confused

Hurt
betrayed
shocked
stunned
aggrieved
abandoned

Learn more at
www.StorytellingLeader.com

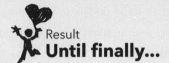

Action
And so... (A choice) And then...

Result
Until finally...

Optional: Do you have data to quantify it? (How much? How big? How fast? How good? Qualitative data?)

Insight / Connection:
And now we know... / And that's why...

Getting ready to build your story

Thousands of leaders around the world have used the Story Canvas to develop their narrative assets. Over and over again, I've seen it improve the quality of their stories to create engagement and belief so people will act. The act of visually constructing their stories on the Canvas invites you to slow down and be more thoughtful—more *strategic*—about why and how you tell your story.

In fact, I thought it would be a good time to once again experience what it was like to build a story on the Story Canvas for myself. I don't use the Story Canvas like I once did, because over time the structure has become much more intuitive for me. I can quickly construct effective stories with a lot less effort than I used to. With deliberate practice, the same will happen for you.

As I constructed the story about Hema on the Story Canvas, I quickly rediscovered just how challenging, clarifying, and deeply engaging the process can be! Take a look at the output of my Story Canvas work on the next spread. You'll see how the details align with the story I actually told about Hema. (You'll also see that the story evolved a bit between the Canvas and how I actually wrote it in this chapter. There are some elements that changed during the telling. We'll talk more about that later.)

Now it's your turn. In this part of the Story Dash, you will construct one of your stories on the Story Canvas.

First, you'll need to choose a story. Select just one of your stories that you identified in the Story Mining exercise. (Yes, you can build the other ones later. One at a time, people.)

Review the sticky notes from your Story Mining now. Select one that you think is especially relevant to this project, or potentially powerful, or just personally urgent for you. Sometimes, there's one story that seems to step forward and present itself and you *just know:* "I need to tell *this* one."

Have you selected one story to develop using the Story Canvas? Good.

There are a few other things you'll need to get started. Of course, you will need a copy of the Story Canvas. You are welcome to photocopy the small version that appears on the previous two pages of this book. However, this process works best if you have the full-sized Canvas printed on 11 × 17–inch paper (or A3 paper in Europe). If you're facilitating this exercise with a team, it is worth the effort to have them printed in advance on high-quality card-stock paper at a nearby print shop. The full-sized version of the Story Canvas can be downloaded as a PDF document at the website www.StorytellingLeader.com.

You'll also need some more yellow "Post-it" sticky notes. You probably already have them next to you, since you used them for your Story Mining. Be sure to get the "classic" sized square notes, since they will fit best on the full-sized Story Canvas.

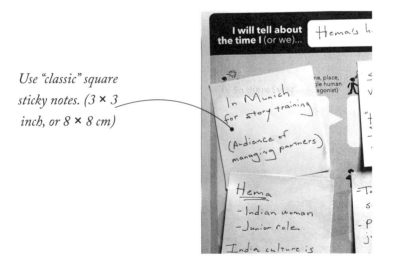

Use "classic" square sticky notes. (3 × 3 inch, or 8 × 8 cm)

Before you get to work building your story on the Story Canvas, let's take a quick walk through the framework. It's important to understand why these elements are there. If you are doing this as a team exercise, share these details with all team members. I explain the Story Canvas elements in a video available at www.StorytellingLeader.com; you can play it for your team if you wish.

I will tell about the time I (or we)... Hema's humble story leads

In Munich for story training

(Audience of managing partners)

She had a vulnerable story

"Human" side of SARS

ostracized

Hema
- Indian woman
- Junior role

India culture is deferential to leadership

- Tough audience of senior / MEN
- Potential for judgement
- Hema is scared

(ne, place, gle human agonist)

or exte goal)

ces, ...)

Sad
depressed
disappointed
regretful dismayed
disillusioned pessimistic
mournful

Mad
frustrated annoyed
defensive
disgusted outraged
offended

Happy
glad overjoyed
relieved
elated
pleased excited
grateful thrilled
content
amused
triumphant

anxious vulne
stressed
nervous ca
confused

Hurt
betrayed
shocke
stunned
aggrieved
abandon

Learn more at
www.StorytellingLeader.com

Action   And then I...
So I/we... And then we...

Leaders were
emotional / wiping
eyes.

"We felt
something shift."

She told her
story!
Nervous /
whispered
Powerful!
"Electric feeling"

New ##
investment in
Bangalore.

Hema's influence
grew!!

Insight / Connection:

Story elements
are powerful,
and ~~transceder~~
transcend bad
"style"

Example of
"neural coupling"

_____

TRUST THE
CARDS! Just
           do it!

A walk through the Canvas

As a first step, simply let your eyes scan the Story Canvas. These boxes that compose the Canvas are the time-tested elements that, collectively, create the connection we are seeking.

Even before I describe any of its content, it already feels kind of like a story, doesn't it? It is intuitive and familiar. You've heard stories that follow this format countless times, and you've never gotten tired of it. Your appetite for story is insatiable. I've used this structure to tell stories all throughout this book, and my guess is that you never thought, *Gosh, these all share a common structure.* The structure is archetypal. When you use it, it's so natural that it is invisible.

I will tell about the time ...

Your first step will be to give your story a title. Perhaps you'll use the same language that you wrote on the sticky note during the Story Mining exercise, or you may wish to update the language.

I titled my story "Hema's humble story leads to investment." Simple enough.

This title is just for you. You won't say the title when you tell the story. That would be kind of weird, right? People usually don't do that.

Even though this is a simple act, it is a powerful thing to name your story.

You are made of stories. You have myriad stories constantly flowing through your brain, and when you name one it's like plucking it from the stream and putting a frame around it. It is now an artifact, ready to be observed.

We do this all the time without even noticing it. When I go home to New Orleans, Louisiana, for the holidays and I haven't seen my brothers for more than a year, we start talking this way over the dinner table: "Hey, remember the canoeing trip disaster that Mom and Dad took us on when we were kids?" And then we all start telling our versions of how we remember that story. That language of "The Canoeing Trip Disaster" is significant. Memory becomes artifact, and with repetition it will become part of the Hutchens family mythology and identity. The more we isolate and name our memories, the more we curate a sort of "story bank" in our minds.[1]

The longer you stay in the work of purposefully identifying and telling meaningful stories, the more populated the "story bank" in your mind becomes. Soon you will become one of those compelling leaders who always seems to have a relevant story to bring a depth of connection to any situation.

Pro tips:

- The title doesn't have to be creative. Just name it something that will help you remember what the story is. You don't need to overthink this step.
- Notice that the Canvas shows you can change the pronoun. The story can be about *me* or *us* or *her* or *them*. Yes, the story doesn't have to be about you; it can be about someone else. The leader's perspective is on "we" more than "me," so most of your stories will be about other people.

---

1 You may even wish to curate these stories externally. I use the note-taking app called Evernote on my smart tablet to capture possible stories for future use. I write them down and give them tags—like "strategy" and "manufacturing" and "North America" and "story"—to make them searchable.

So there I was …

I've seen leaders step up to tell a story … and they somehow don't *quite* get there. One of my program participants stepped up in front of the group and said, "I value open communication. I always have. Ever since I started working here, it has always been a part of my leadership style, and I want you to know you can always drop by my office. I have an open-door policy. So come talk to me whenever you wish. That's my story!"

No, that's not a story. I mean, it's a great thought. But it's not a story.

I see this a lot. Getting into a story space seems like a hard chasm for some leaders to cross.

But it doesn't need to be hard it all. Here's my number one tip for ensuring that your story is, in fact, a story: Start with a time and a place marker. I've done this multiple times throughout this book:

I was with Jeanette's team in Boston last year …

A few months ago, I was working in a coffee shop when I received a message on LinkedIn …

This language, which is temporal and spatial, signals the mind that we are in a narrative space. It is compelling. Think of the times you have been bored by the speaker's endless slides of data, and then he says, "That reminds me of something really wild that happened last week. I was at the airport when … " That language pulls you back in, right?

The other important element to add here is a single protagonist. Make your story be about *somebody*. A person.

The reason I emphasize this is that I work with many smart leaders who are in charge of some deeply complicated projects. They'll tell stories about "my client, a healthcare organization with $4 billion in revenue, with three strategic challenges in the marketplace … "

This won't create the neural coupling connection we're looking for.

We don't feel empathy for the institution. People form empathic connections with other people.

What if your story actually *is* about a $4 billion healthcare organization? We still need a person to represent the institution. Put some skin on it. Try something like this: "Yesterday my phone buzzed at 5:30 in the morning, waking me up, and I saw that it was a call from my client Raj, the SVP of Business Intelligence, and I thought, *Oh, no, this isn't going to be good …*"

Start with a time, place, and protagonist.

Pro tips:

- Give the person a name! A name makes the protagonist more real. You've never met Steve Denning or Elizabeth or Hema (or Raj from just a moment ago). But as soon as I told you their names, there's a good chance you started to generate an image of them in your head. Right?
- Throw in just one or two "sensory" details to paint a picture. I heard my colleague Michael McRay coach one of our program participants, "The story will stick when listeners can *see* it." Elizabeth told us that when Nicolas ran up at the beach, he was wet. Was that critical to the outcome of the story? Probably not. But it *was* critical in inviting you to co-create a picture. Your brain *saw* it, right? Likewise, I told you that Hema had her arms tightly crossed as she spoke. That one detail was enough for your brain to place you in the room, while also suggesting something about her emotional state. You don't need to overdo these details. Just one or two visual or sensory cues will prompt your audience to co-create an image.
- "What if the story is about someone else, and I wasn't there?" This question comes up frequently. Most of your stories *will* be about someone else. You can still place yourself in the story and make it yours. I told Steve Denning's Zambia story. It wasn't my story,

and I wasn't there when it happened. But I put myself into the story by sharing what it made me think about and how I experienced it: "This almost seems too good to be true … but I've seen it happen … "

I wanted … but …

Conflict is the engine that moves your story forward. As you build your story on the Canvas, your first challenge will be to find the conflict in your story.

In my story about Hema, the conflict was that Hema was taking a risk by delivering a vulnerable story to a group of intimidating leaders. (I even heightened the conflict with the implication that they were "mostly men.")

The role of conflict is at the heart of why we, as humans, have developed this capability to tell stories. It's a survival skill that has made our species very successful. Storytelling accelerates a human process called "experience mapping." The idea is that we are all moving through this complex world, which is full of threats and creatures that can eat us and competitors that can take our market share. As we do so, each of us is building a "map" in our mind for moving through this complicated world, helping us to deal with threats so we survive and grow.

So when you tell me a story with conflict in it, you fill in a little piece of my experience map for me. This is incredibly efficient. By telling your story, you have saved the members of your tribe the time and resources and perhaps pain of having to experience it themselves. Your stories make the tribe more resilient, adaptable, and successful. Story is a time-saving technology.

Your story with conflict is interesting at a primal level. It seizes the attention of our 100-million-year-old limbic brain, which is constantly scanning the landscape for threat. When you bring conflict into your story, we will lean forward with interest, ready to update our mental maps.

The recipe for describing your conflict is simple. There is a desire … and a constraint. "There's something we wanted … but there's a reason we couldn't have it."[2]

I've done this all throughout this book.

In my Boston technology team story, I *wanted* this team to believe in the value of telling stories and to trust me as a consultant … *but* they were on a time crunch and didn't want me there.

In the aquarium story (which you will find on the "Us at Our Best" Story Dash Card) the aquarium worker *wanted* to share his love for his work with customers, *but* a request came from a child with autism while the aquarium was closed.

Capture the conflict of your story in the simplest terms possible on your Story Canvas.

Pro tips:

- The conflict doesn't have to be an argument. In a lot of leadership stories, the conflict is *our own mental models and beliefs.* The conflict in your story might be "I didn't like this" or "This didn't match our beliefs, or how we normally do things around here."
- Keep it to just a single conflict. In reality, you will be able to describe *lots* of conflict swirling about any single incident. Resist the temptation to describe all of them (because then you'll be on the hook to *resolve* all of them in the story and that may be more work

---

2 Broadway composers all know that early in their story, the protagonist must establish their motivation by singing an "I want" song. Listen for it in the next musical you see. In Disney's *Little Mermaid*, Ariel sings that she wants to "be part of that world where the people are" BUT she is stuck with fins which means she must live under the sea. In *The Lion King*, Simba "just can't wait to be king," BUT right now he's just a little lion cub and everyone tells him what to do. What's your favorite musical? See if you can identify the "I want" song in the first act.

than your story can bear). You may have noticed the "narrative arc" running across the Story Canvas. Your story should be about "one thing" with a single rising conflict followed by a single resolution.

- "What if I simply can't reduce it to a single conflict?" That may be a sign that you actually have multiple stories to tell. Develop them separately, one at a time, on the Story Canvas. My friend Bill told me a story about a software development project: "The project was plagued with problems. We were answering to too many stake-holders. And we were building the software as an app for teenag-ers and we didn't even understand the teenagers." I stopped him and said, "Wait a minute. I think you have two different stories there: one about managing multiple stakeholders, and one about user-centered design with teenagers. Which one is important?" He said, "They're both important!" So Bill developed two separate sto-ries. Both were brilliant.

And so ... and then ... (choice and action)

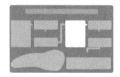

So far we have identified a time, place, and protagonist; and then intro-duced a conflict. We are climbing the "story arc" to the climax of your story. It's time for something to happen, and that something comes in the form of a choice that someone makes:

… and so Hema pushed through her fear and told about her painful SARS experience to a room full of senior leaders.

… and so Elizabeth was crushed at the thought of being a corporate "villain" and committed to working on behalf of her son.

…and so the Little Mermaid, Ariel, went to visit Ursula, the Sea Witch.

… and so Maurice drove from the aquarium gift shop to the little boy's home on a Saturday (from the "Us at Our Best" Story Dash Card).

Often, this part of the story requires a series of actions. "And then … and then …" You'll probably find that your pen will start flying over the page as you describe what happened after that and then what happened after that.

In fact, that flying pen is the thing you'll have to watch out for. The big mistake people make here is throwing in way too much detail.

What is the minimal amount of information that will move the story forward? It may be just a few sentences. You'll be surprised how much your story *doesn't* need.

In my story about Hema, you may have noticed that I did not include the actual story that she told. In a previous draft of my writing, I did include it … but found that quoting her full story was distracting from *my* story, which was more about the energy and "the shift" in the room. So I made some bold edits and removed her telling of her story.

What's the minimum amount of information that will move your story forward?

Pro tip:

- What is the behavior that you wish more people would adopt? Include that behavior in this part of the story! I want you to trust the tools that I'm using in the Story Dash, so I told two stories showing my clients doing just that. (I showed you Elizabeth benefiting from using the Story Deck, and then Hema benefiting from using the Story Canvas, because I want you to conclude, "Hmmm, maybe I should give it a try because I want those great results!") So what is the behavior *you* want people to replicate? Let people see that behavior in the story.

Until finally

I find that most people don't struggle too much with this part of the Story Canvas. Here you answer the question "*So what finally happened?*"

… until finally, the World Bank became a leader in the global knowledge management community.

…until finally, the company invested in the Bangalore facility, and Hema discovered her voice of leadership.

… until finally, Elizabeth was no longer stuck and exercised courage to tell a great story that "cast a spell" over her team and advanced the project.

I've had some leaders get stuck because they say "we're still in the middle of our project, so we don't have an ending yet."

Your project may not have ended, but the *story* can certainly end. Something is different because of the events you just described. Tell us what it is.

This can be a place to bring in some data. While this is optional, in organizational work I find that many leaders do have data to integrate. You might say, "It only cost 50 percent of what our client budgeted," or "The team implemented the six-week plan in just four weeks!" Or "The Boston team won the contract worth $250 million." If you have some data to reference, you may include it here.

Pro tip:

- You can choose to strategically eliminate the ending so that people will feel the tension of incompletion. That's what Steve Denning did brilliantly with his Zambia story. He called it out explicitly: *We aren't in this story. What are you going to do about that?* Now the system was moved to resolve the story tension that Steve had created.

And now we know ... And that's why ...

This is the most important element of your story. At the end of the story, the leader says, "There's a reason I told you this. I think it says something important."

Then you have to say with your words what that thing is. You can't trust that your audience has landed on the conclusion you wanted. They won't. Stories are so rich in meaning, your audience's minds are spinning toward infinitely unpredictable conclusions, until you bring them all together. For Hema's story, I brought you to the conclusion I wanted you to focus on: that a story can create a powerful shared experience that neuroscientists call neural coupling, and that you should desire this powerful connection as a key to your leadership influence.

Most people find this part of the Story Canvas to be challenging. When I work with leaders and teams, it is one of the areas where we spend the most time. What is your story about? The answer is, *whatever you say it is about.* Your choices here are infinite. And this is where your voice of leadership intent steps forward.

The clarifying question here is: What do you want your audience to believe, or to feel, or to do? Identify that belief, feeling, or action, and then name it explicitly when you tell the story.

In Appendix 4, I'll show you more detail about how I have been intentional in selecting stories in this book to achieve specific "believe/feel/do" outcomes.

Pro tips:

- Try completing "And now we know …" first! After you complete this portion of the map, then jump back to the beginning of the map with "So There I Was" and proceed. Completing that last box of the map first will give you important clarity. As you build your story, you'll find it much easier to decide which elements to leave in your story and which to exclude. Does the detail help get you to this strategically chosen conclusion? If not, then it's outta there.

- When you tell your story, you can move "And now we know" to the front. For example, I could have started my story by saying, "Storytelling can create a powerful moment of connection that actually links people's minds together. I met a woman named Hema, who …" This is engaging because now I've signaled what the story is going to be about, and you will be actively listening for how that idea is going to show up in the story. (Note that *all* of the Story Canvas elements are malleable and can be switched around. But for now, we won't go there. Let's get comfortable with the basics before we start doing jazz-riff experimentation.)

- Keep it elegant and clear! Make the "and now we know" just one thing. You'll be tempted to keep milking your story for another insight and then another and then another. I get it. But in our pursuit of elegant clarity, choose the one that is most important and stay with it.

Emotional content/somatic memory

In the lower left corner of the Story Canvas is a pool of emotion words. This pool is not linked to the linear flow of the other story elements. Instead, it has a series of little streams that feed all of the other parts of the Canvas.

You'd be surprised how often I hear leaders tell stories without any emotional content. This is especially true for leaders in engineering, science, or technology contexts who may be more likely to struggle with all of that messy human emotion.

If you were to hear a story without emotional content, it would sound ... flat. You wouldn't like the story. And, further, you wouldn't be able to quite articulate why you didn't like the story unless I pointed out to you "Wow, there was no emotional content in that story," at which you point you would agree and say, "Oh my gosh, you're right!"

Your audience requires this emotional content. Without it, we are like Antonio Damasio's patient Elliot: We won't be able to interpret or assign value to what you are saying because we don't know what it feels like.

If I said to you, "The employee engagement survey results are back," that is a fact. It is a point of data.

Now imagine if I said to you, "The employee engagement survey results are back, and I am completely shocked!"

How did you experience the first statement? How did you experience the second?

The first statement will probably elicit a reaction from you like "Oh, okay."

The second will probably make you say, "Really?! What did it say? Show me!" You felt it as much as you thought it, if not more, and it compelled you to respond.

Remember, we are telling stories to create engagement and belief so people will act. As your audience, I need emotion words. Say the words. Drop them all throughout your story. It can be simple statements:

"Her team felt shamed and ostracized."

"Hema felt proud."

"I'll never forget the disappointment in Nicolas's eyes."

"I was so glad Elizabeth found the courage and changed her mind."

Say the emotion words. Don't shy away from this content. Your audience needs to know what your story *feels* like before they can understand it.

Pro tips:

- You can artfully convey emotion without saying emotion words. In Hema's story, I said that one leader "wiped his eyes." This behavioral description was likely enough for you to conclude he was moved to tears because of the emotional content in Hema's story.

- We already talked about this in the first chapter, but I'll repeat it here. I have many leaders tell me they don't want to "get emotional" by telling a story. I get it. You don't want to compromise your cool leadership style. And you don't have to. You don't have to *show* emotion on your face (if that is uncomfortable to you). But you can still *describe* emotion. I've seen leaders keep a stoic, emotionless face as they've described the "dignity of the team." It's still powerful. At least *say* the emotion words. No one will accuse you of being an "overly emotional American" like me.

- Of course, if you are comfortable doing so, you can certainly display emotion with your facial expressions, tone of voice, and body language. That's definitely a part of my style!

Your turn

Whew! That was a lot of description to walk through the Story Canvas!

Again, if you had skipped this section of the book and simply gone to work on the Story Canvas, you probably could have filled in the boxes without too much help. But since we are building our storytelling agility as leaders, knowing *why* we're doing what we are doing is an important part of our development.

Of course, the other part of that development is action. And that's what comes next. It's your turn. Let's build your story on the Story Canvas.

This is so straightforward, we almost don't need a list of process steps. Just go get some sticky notes, and start dropping them into the Canvas.

Here are a few thoughts, though.

This work goes great with coffee. Go fill up your mug in the break room before you get started. (If you're in a European office, make that a cappuccino … and know that I'm jealous of your high-quality office espresso.)

Get comfortable. It surprised me the first couple of times that leaders would lie on the floor to complete the Story Canvas, but I love it. Find whatever posture facilitates your introspection.

Work quietly and individually. If you are doing this together as a team, give everyone a quiet place to work and reflect.

Allow thirty minutes. Sometimes people complete the Story Canvas in much less time than that because the story springs from their brains completely formed and ready to go. But most people are going to need a full half-hour or more of gestation. Allow yourself generous time to experiment with your story's structure.

Use the sticky notes, which allows you to experiment. Many people, for example, will be in the middle of their Canvas and think, *Oh, wait a minute … maybe this is actually the beginning of the story!* They can remove the sticky note from the middle and reposition it under "So there I was."

How much detail should you put on the Story Canvas? I think this is a matter of personal preference. Personally, I like to capture just a few high-level notes for each story element. This is the minimum amount of content that I want to make sure shows up in each part of the story. (Again, take a look at my example a few pages back to get a sense of my preferred style.) I think that's a great way to go because it prevents me from getting lost in too many details. But I find that some people are detail thinkers and really want to write the entire story out like a script, so they load the Canvas with tiny, dense text. Find your process and make the tool work for you.

You're ready. Begin. When you're done building your story, I'll meet you at the beginning of the next chapter.

The Story Canvas process

1. Print large 11 × 17 or A3 copies of the Story Canvas in advance.

2. This part of the process can be challenging! Have a comfortable workspace. Make coffee or tea, and have snacks available.

3. Have plenty of square sticky notes.

4. Select one story from the previous Story Mining activity to build on the Story Canvas.

5. If you are doing this work with a team, first explain the elements of the Story Canvas. You are welcome to borrow my language from

how I described it in this chapter. Or, you may play the video of me explaining the Canvas, found at www.StorytellingLeader.com.

6. Have all team members work individually.

7. Experiment with your story. Move sticky notes around or delete by crumpling them up.

8. Minimal text on the sticky notes is recommended, but find your preferred style.

9. Allow around 45 minutes for this exercise. That's 15 minutes to introduce the Canvas, and then 30 minutes of building.

Chapter 4:
BREATHING LiFE
via the Tell Test

"I told a story," Sherry told me, "and I don't think it worked. Now I'm feeling weird about it."

"Okay, tell me about that."

"What I'm trying to do," she said, "is spark a culture change where we become more customer focused in the Global Quality function. I was on a call with my team last week and I tried telling a story. But no one said anything. Maybe I did it wrong."

Stories for culture change to become customer focused? Yes!! I love this stuff! (That's not weird, is it?)

Fortunately, the call was recorded, so I could hear her "customer focus in Global Quality" story verbatim. Roll the tape:

> I want to start our conversation today with a little story. Here in Global Quality, we've lost focus on our internal customer and on the value we provide. Last week I was at the Quality Forum in Singapore, and I heard a speaker who told a story about how Starbucks had a similar problem a few years ago. And the story

is, they had lost touch with their customers, so Starbucks closed down all of their stores for a day, which cost them millions of dollars, so they could focus on learning. Soon, we'll be making a significant investment in renewing our focus on the customer as well. In the coming weeks I'll introduce you to Shane G., the consultant who I heard speaking in Singapore. He's the one who told us the Starbucks story. He has worked with some of the biggest companies in the world, and he has agreed to work with us for our culture change effort. I think he will challenge us in all of the right ways.

So that's Sherry's story. Hmmm. Okay. This is interesting.

Before I tell you my opinion, what do *you* think of Sherry's story? If Sherry asked you for coaching, how would you respond?

Spend a few minutes reflecting on this. We'll come back to it.

Breathing life

In the previous step of the Story Dash, you built your story on the Story Canvas. But your work wasn't done, any more than Geppetto's work was done when he first carved Pinocchio from a block of wood. Now we need to animate your story by breathing life into it. Fortunately, this doesn't require a magic spell from the Blue Fairy—just people to tell your story to.

This is a simple process, but it is the central event of the Story Dash. You'll sit in a circle. You'll take turns telling your stories. Then, as a team, you will "workshop" them and make them better.

It's also the most invigorating part of the process. When you bring people together in a circle to take turns telling stories, you engage a timeless structure for meaning making, knowledge creation, and human connection. It's a rich experience. One leader described it to me as "magical."

Be prepared for some surprises. When you tell your story to others, it may sound and feel very different than it did when you built it on the Canvas. That part of the story that seemed so powerful on a sticky note may fall flat when you tell it. On the other hand, you may see the audience's eyes light up at a detail that you didn't think was important.

So, the first objective of the Tell Test is to make your story better by telling it and then receiving feedback about its impact.

There's also another objective, which is to begin building your team's shared story agility. For teams that seek to grow in influence, "preparing the story" becomes an expectation and a priority. They expect to invest some energy and time here. It's a task that gets built into the project plan.

This is the case at Amazon. Remember when we looked at Jeff Bezos's expectation that his leaders would come into strategy meetings with stories? There's nothing superficial about the approach. It's a discipline, and in a letter to shareholders in which he described the practice, Bezos offers a glimpse into how high his expectations are. He says his leaders' stories should "have the clarity of angels singing … brilliant and thoughtful, [the stories] set up the meeting for high-quality discussion."[3]

Some of his leaders, Bezos continues, "mistakenly believe their story can be prepared in one or two days or even a few hours, when really it might take a week or more! The great [story memos] are written and rewritten, shared with colleagues who are asked to improve the work, set aside for a couple of days, and then edited again with a fresh mind."

The clarity of angels singing?

A week of development?!

I can picture Bezos's leaders agonizing and obsessing over the details of their stories prior to the big meeting, knowing they will become the subject of scrutiny from the boss, not to mention the critical foundation for the ensuing strategy work. Bezos has seen the power of story for moving the system and so he's institutionalizing it. To aspire to senior leadership at Amazon is to commit to the journey of building your story agility.

Let's give it a try. I bet your team hasn't had many conversations like the one you're about to have. We're going to wish upon a star, summon the Blue Fairy, and explore how we might breathe life into your stories so they too sing with the clarity of angels.

What is a good story?

You have two roles in the story circle. You will serve as a story teller, and also as a story listener.

The listening role is just as important (if not more important) than the telling role. That's because after telling their story, your team mate is going to look to you and say, "Well, what do you think?" And your role will be to step forward with some coaching and conviction about what makes a good story.

I remember that the great Pulitzer prize–winning film critic Roger

3 You can view the letter at the U.S. Securities and Exchange Commission archive at https://www.sec.gov/Archives/edgar/data/1018724/000119312518121161/ d456916dex991.htm.

Ebert once said that it's not enough to have an opinion that a movie is good or bad. He said you need to know *why* it's good or bad. He was making a case that moviegoers develop literacy around the language of cinema and the mechanics of story, and that's what we are practicing here. For knowledge-era leaders, story literacy is a core competency. Let's get good at this.

Even after doing quite a bit of this work, I still sometimes feel a moment of uncertainty when someone asks, "Hey, David, what did you think of my story?"

Sometimes it's easy. You're going to hear some stories that you just love. You'll definitely know it when you hear it, because you and your team members will all say "Wow! That was awesome! Don't change a thing! You have to tell it again just like that!"

However, more often a storyteller will finish their story and look at you with expectation and ask, "So, what did you think?" and you'll respond the way I did to Sherry's story: "Hmmm. Okay, yeah. Interesting." Pressure's on. You may know that you didn't like the story, but the hard part is providing something generative that will get the story and the teller to a better outcome.

I've been coaching leaders' stories for a while now, and I began my career in advertising where we fixated obsessively on strategic messaging. So I've got a point of view about good storytelling that I've refined over the years. While there are no shortcuts to building world-class narrative coaching ability, I do have some thoughts that can get you to a helpful place of support pretty fast.

When I'm listening to a story for the purpose of providing feedback, I find myself following a specific path that always serves me well. My process when evaluating a story is the following:

- Test clarity of purpose and outcome
- Exercise somatic awareness
- Map it to the Canvas

Test clarity of purpose and outcome

The first question I consider is always around strategic clarity. *Is it clear to me why the leader is telling this story?*

I should be able to discern right away what it is that you want me to *know, feel,* or *do.* I'll test this by asking the teller overtly: "So, did you tell me this story because you wanted me to [have reaction X]?"

But if I have trouble articulating that outcome, then that's where we need to start our conversation. I might even ask the teller to clarify what they wrote in the "And now we know" frame of the Canvas. Then we can evaluate whether the story is serving their intention or not.

Exercise somatic awareness

Story is felt. It is somatic; you experience it in your body. Some story theorists even argue compellingly that the defining characteristic of a story is not its "beginning/middle/end" content, but rather the felt experience it creates for the listener! ("If it didn't create that 'story feeling' then it wasn't a story.")

It is a valuable exercise to direct attention to your body while listening to a story. Pay attention to what you feel, and where. This will become an important part of the feedback you give to the teller. After all, our ultimate goal is for your audience to be moved, right? To evaluate the impact of the story, we must learn to notice and diagnose that impact on ourselves.

I listen to many leaders share their messages, and I have become more and more attuned to the movement between my thoughts (which I can feel moving around "up there" in the squishy folds of my brain) and my emotions, which shows up as a bodily sensation, often in my chest area. In a good presentation I can actually feel that energy moving back and forth: Brain, body. Thought, emotion. "Hm, okay, interesting … OH WOW."

In average or uninspiring leadership presentations (which is to say most of them), I can feel that we are parked "up there" in the brain the entire time and at the end I have this strong awareness that, while the content may have been smart, I just never *felt* anything. In fact, as you'll discover in the next chapter, staying "in the brain" too long is physically tiring and guaranteed to eventually lose your audience. It will also leave them with a head full of information that will evaporate within hours of the message.

I like to be specific in reporting my reactions: "Elizabeth, the moment when you described how you could feel Nicolas's disappointment, that really grabbed me. It made me think of my own son, and that was especially powerful. I actually felt my heart sink a bit … and that's when I really felt the urgency for your project." Sometimes, I will even ask around, "Did anybody else feel that?" and usually everyone nods their heads: Yes, we were all neurally coupled and felt the same thing at the same time.

"Somatic awareness" is a discipline that takes some practice, but it is a powerful way of knowing and of gathering data from the world around you. The next time you listen to a story, direct some of your attention to the felt experience in your body. Be prepared to report when you felt something, what story content generated that response, and the influence you think it would have on you as a member of the intended audience.

Map it to the Canvas

So far, I've clarified the purpose of the story. I've checked myself for somatic impact. If after completing those steps I'm still feeling confused or disconnected from the story, this next step will help illuminate what's going on.

The memory of the Story Canvas is probably fresh in your mind, right? Use it! See if you can quickly map the story you heard to the Canvas. It truly is a clarifying framework, and one sign of a compelling story is that you can practically check off the elements: "Yep, there's the *time and place marker*. Okay, I see the *protagonist*. Wait a minute, did I miss the *conflict*? I'm not sure what it was!"

(Note: Don't get too stuck on sequence! No, the elements of the story do not have to appear in the order that they appear on the Canvas. Artful storytellers can move the elements around, so that the middle of the story is at the beginning, for example. Stories are fluids, not solids.)

If there's a part on the Canvas that you can't quite pick up in the story, ask the teller to clarify it. I say things like, "Maybe it's just me, but I think I

Have a single "arc"
Are you squeezing multiple narratives into your story? Give the story a single conflict and outcome, where "one thing happens."

Put us right there in the action
"So there I was in my office, when suddenly someone is pounding at my door and I'm thinking, *Who in the world is that?*"

"Box car" mini-stories together
Do you have a big or complicated story to tell? Break it down into a series of mini-stories. Think of "scenes" in a movie. Build one mini-story at a time.

Make your story better!

Don't be afraid to go "small"
Your work is complex and big. But it's made of little moments. So tell us about a single conversation. One email. A simple gesture from a team mate. Your story doesn't have to be "epic." Small moments can say everything about who we are!

Use dialogue
Instead of "my manager told me to pack a suitcase," bring the scene to life with dialogue: "My manager Kelly goes, '*Raj, how fast can you get your suitcase packed?*' And I said, '*Are you serious?*'"

Say emotion words
These are the heart of your story! When you say emotion words, the audience will feel those emotions. *The client was excited. Kelly was so surprised. I went to my team and said, "Guys, I'm really puzzled…"*

Keep it brief
Leadership narrative is fast and purposeful. If you follow the structure, you should be able to tell your story powerfully in less than two minutes.

Consider the "five-sentence structure":

1. Situation: "So there I was..."
2. Problem: "I wanted... But..."
3. Action: "So we... And then..."
4. Result: "Until finally..."
5. Leadership insight: "I think this says something..."

Map it to the Canvas
You should be able to check off the Story Canvas elements: "Yes, there's a *time and place* marker... there's the *conflict...*" If it's not clear to the listener, clarify that element and then try telling the story again.

Say their names!
Instead of saying "my manager," say "my manager, Kelly." Simply saying the name will make the audience create an image in their mind. (Do this only when confidentiality is not an issue.)

missed the conflict. When you built your story on the Canvas, how did you articulate that?" Or, "Who would you say was the protagonist in your story? You started by talking about Dr. Clements, but then suddenly it was all about the young radiologist and I got confused." Often, when they clarify their intent, I find myself saying, "Oh, that makes a lot of sense when you put it like that! But that didn't come through when you told the story. How might we say it so the audience doesn't miss it like I did?"

A cheat sheet

Finally, I've developed a one-page document that I share with my teams to use as a "cheat sheet" to support them in coaching one another. The page is called "Make Your Story Better," and it quickly summarizes the most common reasons that good stories go bad. This is the feedback that I found myself giving to teams most often. Because I was repeating these tips so frequently, I thought, *Maybe I should just write it down and hand it out to people*. No, this page won't fix every problem. But it will hit on the ones that send your story into the ditch most often. You can view the handout on the facing page, and you can download it in PDF format at www.Story tellingLeader.com.

Now let's do a quick run-through of Sherry's story using my coaching lenses:

- **Strategic clarity**: This is the one piece that I picked up with no problem. Sherry laid out the point of her story to me clearly: to spark a culture change in which Global Quality sees itself as a customer service organization. As soon as she said that, I started listening closely for that payoff. Now I'm able to go through each element of the story and evaluate whether it illuminates that intent or not. Already I'm getting some ideas on how I need to respond.
- **Somatic awareness**: When I heard her story (and when I reviewed it a second time), I get almost no emotional response. I "felt" it parked up in my head the whole time. I never got that moment when I felt it in my emotions. (Did you?)

- **Story Canvas**: As I start mapping her story, I become confused. Something doesn't fit. There are too many elements that aren't helping the story. I'm looking for that "single arc," and that's when I realize that she has confused her message by squishing two stories together.

Okay, I'm ready to give her some feedback.

Coaching Sherry's story

I asked you to think about how you would coach Sherry. What would you say? Read her story again, and then take a few minutes to write down a few thoughts before you read mine. Do that now. I'll wait.

If we were in the same room, I would make you go first with your insights so you could practice giving story feedback. But speaking back to the author remains (for now) a limitation of book technology.

So I'll venture forth, starting with what I liked:

The strategic clarity was there

Sherry knew why she was telling her story. She said she wants to introduce a culture change in which Global Quality becomes a customer-focused organization. A single, clear outcome. Got it. She's doing something similar to what Steve Denning did with his Zambia story; it's an "imagine if we had that here" story, which is one of the "novelty" stories on the Story Dash Cards.

A lot of leaders struggle to get to this level of simple purpose clarity, but Sherry got there decisively. We are off to a good start.

She's on to something with the Starbucks story

The Starbucks illustration was immediately interesting to me. I had never heard that story, so I Googled it to get more detail. Wow. The Starbucks "close all the stores to refocus" case study just got better and better the more I read. I can see how it could connect to her strategic intent.

Between her clear intent and the cool Starbucks story asset, she has the raw materials to create a powerful message!

However, there were some things that hurt her story:

Don't say the "S" word

I'm glad to get this one out of the way first. This isn't just feedback for Sherry; almost everyone makes this mistake.

Don't say the word "story." It surprises groups when I tell them this, because we've been talking about stories all day long and I've probably said the word "story" hundreds of times.

Have you ever heard a speaker step up to begin their presentation and they say, "I just want to begin with a little story ..." and you think, *Ugh, okay, sure, whatever, let's get on with it.* I do. There's something about saying "I want to tell you a story" that breaks the spell. It calls attention to the device.

On the other hand, if Sherry had simply started her message by saying "Last week I was at the Global Quality conference in Singapore ..." no one would have thought, *Oh, she's hoping to create engagement with narrative!* It would sound like she was just talking to us. When you do it right, story is invisible. It's stealth technology. It's the most natural way of speaking and no one knows you're using a device unless you tell them you are.

So don't say the "S" word.

She used no emotion words

Did you notice that? Go back and look again. Sherry didn't use a single emotion word. I can imagine that this story fell flat when she told it on her call because she hasn't indicated how the audience is supposed to feel. Should we be *amazed* at the bold move Starbucks made? Should we be *saddened* that we've lost touch with our internal customer? Should we be *cautiously excited* at this opportunity? It was hard to interpret what her story was supposed to feel like because we didn't have the context of emotional data. A few simple emotion words would go far in supporting our sensemaking.

Give us a single arc (and focus on Starbucks)

It took me a few minutes to realize that the reason I felt so muddled was that Sherry has mashed two different stories together. There's the story of meeting Shane the consultant (and the message that he'll be working with us); and then the Starbucks story. She should choose one and commit to it.

She said this story needs to be about creating a customer-focused culture, and I think the Starbucks story is clearly the way to get there. I wanted more! I even felt a little cheated that the details were so sparse in the "And so …" portion of the Starbucks story. I found myself going, *Wait a minute … what did Starbucks do?* You've hooked me, Sherry. Lean into the Starbucks story and trust it to do the work for you.

Give us a human (and different) protagonist

As I checked through the Story Canvas, I found myself confused as I tried to map Sherry's story to the very first box (time, place, and protagonist), and I can see why. The story started being about Shane, but then it wasn't about Shane. Now that we've decided to pursue the Starbucks story, we know Shane G. isn't our protagonist. We need another protagonist "with skin on them." After Googling the story, it was clear that the "close the stores" strategy was driven by their iconoclastic CEO at the time, Howard Schultz. There's our protagonist. Let's put him in the story and see if it feels different.

Ditch the consultant!

I confess that my heart sank a bit when Sherry closed her story with "I'll introduce you to our consultant, Shane." A consultant? Really!? Ugh! I'm sure Shane is awesome, but that's not where this story of culture change needs to land. You're inviting the team on a journey, and they need to see themselves in the story.

I'm always listening for an *invitation*. How will you move the audience forward? What do you want your audience to feel, believe, or do? Inviting your team to take a bold step into a change journey is so much more engaging than "we're paying someone to save us." I recommend removing Shane from this story, instead putting the spotlight on the team with an invitation to act. (If Sherry does need to build a case that they are engaging a consultant, that's a different message, a different outcome … and a different story.)

Take two: Sherry's return

That was my coaching. Sherry was a great sport, did some more work, and came back with round two of her story. I think it landed in a much better place! Check it out:

> What do you think it would take for us in Global Quality to re-imagine ourselves as a *customer service organization*? I was surprised to learn that Starbucks faced this challenge as well! A few years ago, their CEO, Howard Schultz, realized to his horror that their growth was hurting their connection to their customers. As Starbucks stores became busier, their employees were no longer having the same authentic conversations that their customers loved in the beginning. He even saw that the new cappuccino machines were bigger than the old ones and blocked eye contact between baristas and customers. Not good! So Schultz did something that shocked everybody: He closed down every one of their stores in North America for half a day of training. Can you believe that? It cost millions of dollars! And he made sure his customers knew why: "Our team is refocusing on serving you better!" Even though customers had to go a morning without their grande mocha lattes, they loved it, and it was the beginning of a dramatic turnaround for Starbucks. I wonder how we are like Starbucks? We all came to this team because we believed in the value that Quality Control brings to our company, but we've lost "eye contact" with our internal customers.

Where have we drifted? And what would it look like if we made a powerful statement of recommitment to the people we serve? I would love to hear your ideas about that!

Nice! The Starbucks story has an element of the unexpected and provides a credible case study for a decision to disrupt the business; it is a great "imagine if we did that here" vision story. Referencing "eye contact" with the internal customer was a smart callback to the cappuccino machine metaphor.

I especially love the questions she asks at the end: What would it look like if we did something like that? I always tell people that a story is never the end of a conversation. It is always the beginning of a conversation: *What do you think the story means? What do you take from this? What ideas for action does it give you? Let's talk!*

The Tell Test process

Structurally speaking, it's simple.

1. Bring together your team members who have each developed a story on the Story Canvas.

2. If you did this work by yourself, then go grab one or two colleagues or friends. Tell them what you've been working on, and explain this process.

3. Sit in a circle. Three to five people is ideal. Use multiple circles if you have larger groups.

4. Push away from the conference room table if possible. Fully face each other, with no tables or barriers between you. (If it's a nice day, this a great conversation to have outside in the sunlight.)

5. Invite one team member to tell their story. Listen fully.

6. Provide coaching to make their story better:

   - Reconnect to purpose.

- Practice somatic awareness.
- Map it to the Story Canvas.
- Use the "Make Your Story Better" handout.

7. Have a conversation with the team and help make the story better.

8. If this is a team exercise, repeat the process: The next person will tell their story and receive support. You'll also have a turn to tell your story and receive the wisdom of your team mates.

9. For a team of four people, expect this process to take about an hour, although it is so invigorating you may find yourselves wanting to invest more time.

Great job!

Congratulations! If you have been facilitating the Story Dash in a disciplined way with an eye on the clock, then you've been working hard for about four or five hours! Treat yourselves to lunch or to a break. Share appreciation for the gifts that your team mates brought to the process.

Most importantly, refine your stories. Connect them to your message. And then breathe life into them by telling them to your intended audience.

Chapter 5:
ACTIVATE! STORY, DATA, and the 30 PERCENT HYPOTHESIS

If you followed the Story Dash process, right now you have a strategically selected, well-developed story that is ready to tell.

If you completed this process with your team, you have several stories that are ready to tell—presumably one for each member of the team (except for that one guy who had to leave early because of a client emergency).

Furthermore, you have a bank of *lots* of stories on yellow sticky notes that you identified in the Story Mining process but have not yet developed.

Since we are taking inventory of where we stand, let's not overlook that you also have a burgeoning new skill set and agility as a storytelling leader. Each additional trip you take through the Story Dash process will become a little smoother and a little faster as you grow more and more confident in the work. Your authentic, "most human" voice of leadership and influence will continue to grow.

So what's next? We bring it to the work.

You will almost never tell your stories in isolation. They will show up in the context of some other activity: A pitch for new business or a sales call. The meeting to unveil the new strategy. A long-overdue update to the stale "About Us" page on your website. A "state of the business" update to your CEO or the Board. A job interview. A fundraising appeal. A speech to the new graduates. An appeal to your team to take the first brave step into your new future together.

Here, we are stepping outside of the "dash" part of our process and into the marathon of activating our new skill across the work that we care most about. This part isn't fast. It is the ongoing learning journey that is outside of the four-hour promise you see on the cover of the book. (Guarantee is limited! Restrictions may apply!)

How do we start activating these story assets to bring movement to your most urgent leadership imperatives?

When I'm working with a team, the question often sounds a little different. People say things like, "Hey, listen, David, today's been great—really inspiring—and I love what you're saying, so don't get me wrong. But I don't want to overdo this story stuff, you know? I mean, my client has explicitly asked me to review the data with them and I can't only tell stories. Let's be honest, story can't be the answer to everything. How much story is too much?"

Hey, it's cool. I hear you. Now that we are thinking about tomorrow morning when we are back at work and actually facing the task of applying the "story stuff" we've been talking about, a bit of doubt can start to creep in.

In her book *The Fearless Organization*,[1] Dr. Amy Edmondson writes about her research at Harvard around the idea of "psychological safety," and she describes the human sensitivity for "impression management." That is, we are highly attuned to how other people perceive us and are deeply sensitive to anything that might affect our standing within a social order. Don't be surprised when your new storytelling awareness makes your "impression management regulator" go haywire: *What if this flops? What if it sounds weird? What if my client judges me? What if I'm the only one on my team who is showing up in this different way? What if I overdo it?*

I promise you it won't be weird. You won't overdo it. It's all about the balance.

....

1 Amy Edmondson, *The Fearless Organization: Creating Psychological Safety in the Workplace for Learning, Innovation, and Growth* (New York, NY: Wiley, 2018).

How much story is too much?

Of course story isn't the "answer to everything." Yes, it is possible to overdo this. How much is too much?

I have long held it as a rule of thumb that around 30 percent of your communication as a leader should be story. I'm not even sure where I got that number. It always felt "about right" to me.

Does "30 percent story" sound right to you? Does it sound high? It makes me wonder about my own communication as a leader. Am I telling stories 30 percent of the time?

I kept getting the "how much is too much" question, and after a while I just got embarrassed that I didn't have a way to justify my 30 percent belief. So I set out to test my hypothesis.

How does one test something like that? I thought a good place to start would be with TED Talks. TED is, after all, an enormously popular platform for communicating innovation messages. And TED talks are famous for being story driven.

I stopped by the TED website and found a page that listed the top TED talks of all time. The most popular talk remains (for a few years now) one that is titled "Do Schools Kill Creativity?" It's the top talk by a landslide. Delivered by a British creativity expert named Sir Ken Robinson, it has been viewed more than 60 million times (as of this writing).

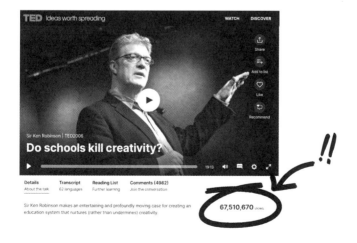

If you haven't viewed it, you should. It's a master class in engaging communication. But my objective here is not to get drawn in by Robinson's wit and engaging presence all over again; I'm testing my 30 percent hypothesis. How might I go about that? I started by creating a transcript of his nineteen-minute presentation, and then placing that content into a spreadsheet—one row for every sentence that Robinson speaks. I then evaluated each sentence, one at a time, to determine if he was telling a story or speaking more didactically. (For the purposes of this exercise, I'm using the term "didactic" to mean "the opposite of story." Think of a college professor lecturing about a theory. It's a "telling" approach that is the norm for most leadership communication.)

I've done these analyses on many communications and the final report can be several pages long. I'll spare you the geeky details; here is a glimpse of the first page of my report from Robinson's TED talk.

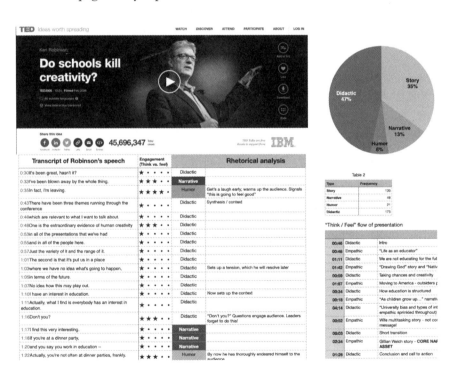

The third column is where you can see my "narrative versus didactic" analysis.

Now I can add up the time, crunch the data, and create a visual time map of Robinson's "Do Schools Kill Creativity?" where the blue bars are story/"feel" language and the gray bars are didactic/"think" language. It looks like this:

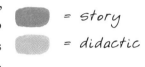

= story

= didactic

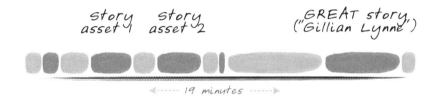

Already you can see a clear pattern in this nineteen-minute presentation, alternating between story (blue) and didactic (gray) communication.

What my simplified map *doesn't* quite show you is how smart Robinson's structure is: Each story (with the exception of some jokes he tells at the beginning) is presented to illuminate the didactic/theoretical presentation that follows.

Or to put it another way, there are three clear points that Robinson wants you to take from his presentation, and he makes those points unforgettable by embedding them in expertly crafted stories.

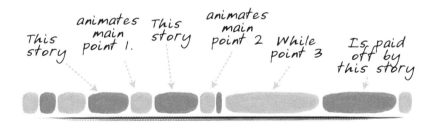

Later you will forget all of the "gray bar" content, but you'll remember his "blue bar" story content. All of this is by design. Robinson knows what he is doing.

What are the critical few messages you want to stick with your audience, so that your organization, system, or market will carry it with them? Get clarity on those takeaways. Then embed them in stories.

The last story, by the way, is a classic, and I suspect might be a big part of the reason this video has tens of millions of views. The way he tells the "Gillian Lynne" story is a blockbuster. I found myself nearly persuaded that schools may, in fact, be killing creativity! If you haven't seen it, I won't ruin the Gillian Lynne story for you. Go watch it and be moved.

I still haven't answered my original question. Is Robinson's persuasive message composed of 30 percent storytelling?

If I push all of the "blue bar" stories together and add them up, "Do Schools Kill Creativity?" has ten minutes total of storytelling across its nineteen-minute run time. That lands at a whopping 53 percent story content.

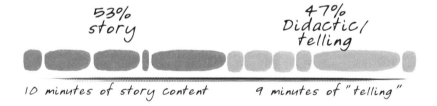

On our very first test of our hypothesis, we've landed significantly *higher* than our proposed 30 percent target.

I showed this to Tom, a pharmaceutical leader I've been working with, and he said, "Well, yeah, but that's a TED Talk. They are supposed to be entertaining! That's different from what we are trying to do here in our bioscience organization."

I challenged him: "Are you sure? I think the TED-style platform is a compelling model for leaders of all kinds to aspire to."

Tom was still resistant: "Well, but Ken Robinson is a master speaker. Someone that good can get up to 53 percent."

Okay. Maybe that's a fair point.

So I looked at the next several TED talks on the "top ten" list (which includes the classic "How Great Leaders Inspire Action" by Simon Sinek, the one where he famously presents his "start with why" principle).

I won't show you all of them, but here is a map of the Sinek talk:

That's a twenty-minute presentation with six minutes of stories. Sinek is right at 30 percent.

This presentation, by the way, currently stands at 51 million views. Yeah, it's good.

Similarly, the number three and four spots on the TED top ten list (including Dr. Amy Cuddy on the topic of presence and body language; and Dr. Brené Brown on the power of vulnerability) also land squarely at 30 percent storytelling; and in different ways are also smart about animating their primary message points by embedding them in the stories.

I've analyzed many other examples of persuasive communications from organizational, political, and system transformation contexts … and (Sir Ken Robinson aside) "30 percent story" receives validation, over and over again. It may indeed be the golden ratio.

Am I practicing what I preach?

What if I applied this analysis to myself and to my work on this *Story Dash* book? When I embarked on writing this manuscript, I started with an explicit goal that I wanted to use stories to advance the ideas. (Maybe that sounds obvious, but you'd be shocked how many story practitioners talk about or write books about storytelling without ever telling stories!)

However, I never assigned myself a 30 percent goal. I've simply followed my intuition, placing stories where I thought they were needed to amplify my messages. I started collating the content of my manuscript, unsure where I might land in my analysis.

Here's the map of Chapter 1. Remember those stories? Ah, those were some good times we had together.

Perhaps you can see how I've used the stories intentionally to make the primary ideas of the chapter compelling and "sticky." (Again, I'll make my strategies around this overt in Appendix 4.)

And here's the map of Chapter 2:

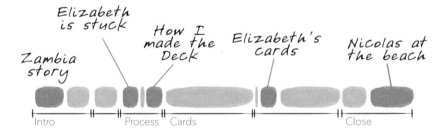

I added up the word counts for both, crunched the numbers, and *boom*: 30 percent. Chapters 1 and 2 both landed almost exactly at our hypothetical ideal. I didn't analyze Chapter 3 or beyond because I have only so much tolerance for this and my wife, Robbie, was calling for me to walk the dog.

I maintain that the 30 percent hypothesis, while not proven as an axiom, stands as a plausible way to approach your most important communication.

My point here is not to convince you that you should analyze the content and count the words of your messages like I did so you can hit an ideal of 30 percent stories. Rather, it is to give you confidence that you have a lot of room to experiment with this! Most of the leaders I work with are somewhere between 0 percent and 5 percent story in their messages.

For those of you who are worried about "overdoing this stuff," my prediction is that you're nowhere close to a 30 percent threshold. You have plenty of room to work with.

So, play. Experiment. Tell one story. See what kind of reaction you get.

If you don't get the response you hoped for, don't conclude "it doesn't work." Instead, ask for feedback and update your story. Then try it again.

Keep going. Add another story.

If it's a really good one, who knows? You might get 60 million views, too.

Attention is on a dimmer switch

I was sitting in the back row of a darkened corporate auditorium listening to a bad presentation. It would be a stretch to say that this senior leader at this consumer products company in Ohio was "speaking to" us, because he was mostly just reading his slides out loud. Loaded with bullet points, diagrams, and data, it was one of those strategy presentations where, twenty minutes in, I still didn't understand the strategy.

I surveyed the audience. I could feel the restless energy. People were starting to shift in their seats. More than a few had their cell phones out and were responding to emails or maybe checking their social media. Oh, they tried to hold their phones down low in their laps so they wouldn't get caught, but I could see the glow.

The worst part was, the speaker on the stage had been in my program the day before. I was trying to communicate with him by telepathy: *Come on, man! You're losing us! Tell a story!*

Maybe it worked, because at that moment he said, "That reminds me of something funny that happened. So there I was, back in my office last week when …"

Yes! Did you recognize the time and place marker? Folks, we've got us a story.

The change of energy in the room was almost immediate. Heads that had been down in their phones suddenly looked up. Postures straightened. I too felt my attention suddenly tugged back toward the stage.

He got his audience back.

I write about these ideas and I talk about them in my programs, and I still have to chuckle a bit when I actually experience it. This stuff still works on me, every time. It works on you, too.

That's because your brain is a hungry organ. As Nobel prize–winning psychologist Daniel Kahneman shows us,[2] thinking is hard, and it consumes a lot of energy. This is why you are physically exhausted after you've worked on a tough problem at work all day even though you didn't move away from your desk. It's why your teenager doesn't want to study for the chemistry exam and instead you catch him binge-watching movies on his laptop. Don't get too mad at your teen; it's biological. Our brains have evolved to attempt to conserve as much energy as possible.

Data is exhausting. Story feels good.

I've come to think of attention as being like a dimmer switch. At our house we have a little dial on the wall that controls the chandelier over the dinner table. We can turn the light up nice and bright; or we can turn the dial and lower the light if we want a romantic meal (which, come to think of it, we haven't done in *forever*. Note to self).

Story resets the dimmer switch of attention. When we first started listening to the strategy presentation in Ohio, we were bright and attentive

....

2 Daniel Kahneman, *Thinking, Fast and Slow* (New York, NY: Farrar, Straus and Giroux, 2011).

with anticipation. The dimmer switch was at its highest setting. But after a while (and about a dozen slides), fatigue set in and our attention began to dim.

Then when the speaker told his story, he reset the switch on our dimming attention. Our tired brains took a rest while we experienced the story, and that two-minute story was enough for our attention to return to its brightest setting. He pulled us back in. Now we were re-engaged and able to focus on the next round of data slides.

My non-scientific observation of many audiences around the world is that people start showing signs of fatigue after around five to nine minutes of hard brain work.

Here's my hypothesis: I think two minutes of story will "buy" you up to nine minutes of attention for your data/theoretical/didactic/"telling" information. (Are there any neuroscience researchers out there who are willing to partner to test this out with some EEGs or fMRIs?)

After around nine minutes of your slides and your explanations, your audience will be feeling fatigue. You should be in the mindset of "I need a story right about now."

In fact, for this chapter for *Story Dash* that is loaded with graphs and talk of "hypothetical ideals," I know I'm flirting with the danger zone. I don't want to lose you. You may have noticed I'm peppering this chapter with stories (such as the "Tom is skeptical about TED Talks" mini-story) to ease you through it. That's because every two minutes of story buys me up to nine more minutes of your attention so I can present my theories.

In fact, nine minutes may be on the more demanding side. In "Do Schools Kill Creativity?" Ken Robinson never goes longer than *four* minutes without reclaiming attention by telling a story:

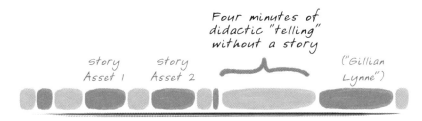

In Sinek's speech, the longest span between stories is three minutes.

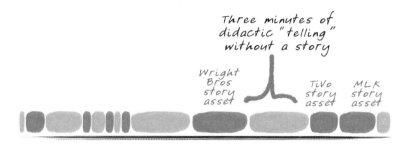

In Chapter 1 of this book, the last section represents around six minutes of reading without a story. (My word processing software estimates this based on word counts and average reading speeds.)

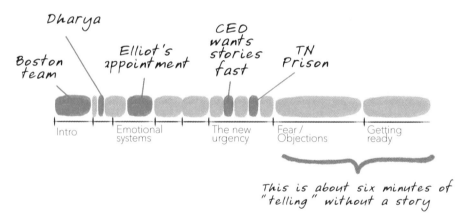

In Chapter 2, you never go more than five minutes of reading without a story.

And so on. You get the idea.

Do you love your message? Do you love your audience? Then honor both with the gift of stories, strategically placed to breathe life into your key takeaways while carefully balancing the think/feel ratio.

Here's where we've landed

As you think about creating engagement and belief in your message to motivate people to act, consider:

What are the two or three points you want your audience to remember?
You're thinking, *But I have eleven important points!* Nope. If your goal is message retention, three is all you get.

How can you breathe life into each of those points with its own story?
You can use a Story Dash to identify and develop your narrative assets that animate those few points and move the audience to the outcomes you desire.

How will you alternate "blue bars" and "gray bars?"
Alternate stories and data. Put your slides, data, theory, and didactic/ "telling"/"gray bar" content in between the stories.

How will you manage content so that you do no more than nine minutes of "telling"?
Test your message by saying it out loud. Use a timer. Are you in theory/ data/didactic for more than nine minutes? You risk losing your audience. Find a story.

 Then practice.
 Exercise your voice.
 Show us who you are.
 Make us believe.

Epilogue: SOMETHING OLDER than the TIDES

Becca Stevens is one of the best storytelling leaders I know. She built her nonprofit organization, Thistle Farms, into a globally lauded center of recovery for women survivors of prostitution, trafficking, and addiction. Today the survivor community of Thistle Farms is learning to be a leadership community, and they are producing and selling millions of dollars' worth of home, bath, and body products. They also run a restaurant and coffee shop that is always buzzing with an engaged crowd of Nashville families, music celebrities, wedding parties, politicians, and more.

Becca built the organization on stories. "Stories are at the core of how we heal, and how we grow the movement," she told me.

Growing movements is one of the things Becca Stevens does best. Her network of partners extends all over the globe, creating opportunities for women survivors of genocide, poverty, immigration, and more. For the past few years I've been supporting Thistle Farms as a member of their board of directors. Spend even a little time around Becca, and I bet you'll find yourself enlisted in the movement too.

Becca, do you have a story for us?

Dorris is one of the great survivor-leaders of Thistle Farms. When she was a child, Dorris witnessed the murder of her father. As a young woman she treated her trauma with drugs and ended up trapped in a ten-block radius on the streets of Nashville for 26 years where she walked and sold herself. When I met Dorris what I saw was a woman filled with equal parts hope and fear.

Two years later, when we traveled to speak to a group in Florida, Dorris told me she had never seen the ocean. We got up as the sun rose and I was privileged to witness the first time her feet touched the sugar sands and experience the amazing grace of feeling found. As she felt the pull of the tide for the first time, she raised her hands to the sky and said, "Has this been doing this my whole life?"

As long as the moon has been spinning around the earth, the tide has been coming in. The only thing more powerful and older is love. Sometimes it just takes a community to help us get to the shore—to feel its power and remember the source.

I've heard Becca tell the "Dorris at the beach" story enough times (as well as others that are just as powerful) that sometimes instead of watching her I like to watch the audience. There is always a physical and behavioral response: Some people take deep breaths, while others might wipe their eyes.

But there's something else that happens that is hard to describe. There's a specific energy as the room becomes very still. There is a phenomenon that I've heard my colleague Paul Costello call "narrative transport" that happens when people deeply enter a story… even to the point of losing some awareness of their surroundings. I often sense that Becca's stories are leading listeners more deeply inside themselves, where they are encountering something that is older and more powerful than the tides.

The fact that the group is having this experience collectively only adds to the power. I remember a few years ago I was at the International Storytelling Festival here in my home state of Tennessee. It is the biggest story gathering in the world, located in the beautiful Smoky Mountain town of Jonesborough. Tens of thousands of visitors gather under giant hillside tents, enveloped by the oranges and yellows of October, to face a stage that is occupied only by a single stool, a microphone, and a teller of stories. I remember watching an audience transfixed by one storyteller, with everyone gasping or laughing all at the same time, and having the strong sense that the crowd had become a single organism.

Perhaps this talk of *love* and *single organisms* is where I'm losing you. "Dude, I'm just trying to sell technology solutions to the financial sector." Yeah, I know. That's the whole idea of this book. You and other readers have picked it up because you have an immediate business need. You need to sell your offerings, or build your culture, or move people to act on your strategic initiatives. That's worthy work, and I've made it my career to support it.

But when we choose to access the ancient technology that is story for our business outcomes, there is something significant happening that I don't want us to miss.

Bobette Buster is a story consultant and lecturer who has worked with movie studios such as Pixar, Disney, 20th Century Fox, and others. "Cinema is the art form of transformation," she told me, and she says people will always be drawn to stories because, ultimately, we are all seeking the answers to three questions for our lives:

Will I find hope?

Will I find transformation?

Will I find transcendence?

At some level, you and I and the financial technology sales guy were drawn to our roles because we too are driven by these questions. We want our world to be better. We want to believe that things won't stay the way they are and that wholeness and transformation are possible in ourselves and in our communities. We want to be delivered from the mundane ways we feel much of the time and experience something greater and truer.

Know that when your audience leans forward to hear your stories of sales or strategy or branding or culture, these are the deeper currents that are pulling them. The more directly you speak to these questions, the more powerful your leadership becomes.

You and other leaders come to a Story Dash because you have some business objective or a task in your role description that you are charged to execute. We've got you covered. Many participants in this process find the great sales or strategy story they were looking for, say "Thanks for the program," and go on their way.

But sometimes you'll get more. You may find yourself surprised by glimpses of something that is deeply human. Participants have reported this in different ways:

"I feel like I'm bringing my voice for the first time."

"What happened here today felt powerful, and I need to think about it."

"This reminded me why I was excited about this work when I was young, and why I got into this business to begin with. I liked feeling that hunger again."

"We felt something shift in the room."

"It's like I discovered a different kind of intelligence I didn't know I had."

"This was profound."

I hope you will stay in the work of telling business stories. Often we stand at this shore with a fishing line in the water, hoping to catch something that will advance our work and feed us for dinner. But sometimes you may feel the pull of an ageless tide that wants to connect you to something deeper and truer, and you too will realize it has been doing this your whole life.

Please support Thistle Farms at www.ThistleFarms.org. Your purchase or donation will help light a path for the next woman to come in from the street.

Appendices

Appendix 1:
THE STORY DASH CARDS
Stories of Continuity, Novelty, and Transition

The six Story Dash Cards are described in Chapter 2: "Story Mining." You may review them on the following pages.

For best results, you should have a copy of these cards printed on heavy paper stock and trimmed so that you can sort and sequence them.

You can download a print-ready file of the Story Dash Cards at www.StorytellingLeader.com.

Continuity

Novelty

Transition

It Was True at the Beginning
"There's something special about how we began."

Ever noticed how every super hero has an *origin story*? To understand them, you have to know how they began.

That's true in organizations, too. These stories hold the DNA of identity, and telling those stories creates powerful continuity.

The origin doesn't have to be the founding of the organization. When you stepped into your current job or new position, there was an origin story. Every time you kick off a new project, you have an opportunity for a origin story.

Find your story!

Tell me about something that happened at the beginning, and what that says about us that is still true.

Front

Example of *It Was True at the Beginning*
"Francisco's Garden"

Our founder, Tami, started her career as a teacher. She worked in the public schools, and she saw the poor nutrition that kids were getting at school. It broke her heart.

One night she was invited to stop by the home of one of her young students, Francisco. She saw the entire family eating potato chips and other junk food for dinner.

Tami said she couldn't believe it. No wonder kids like Francisco were struggling so much!

So she started the first vegetable garden as a class project, so that her students could take home fresh, organically grown spinach and tomatoes to their families. Francisco and the other kids were so proud to eat food that they had grown themselves!

That was ten years ago. Today we have greenhouses in 11 counties, helping dozens of communities manage their own gardens.

Because of the economy, our funding is down and we are making tough choices. But our mission is alive! We believe in bringing food security to every kid in America. And that commitment is one thing that will never change.

StorytellingLeader.com

Back

Continuity
Novelty
Transition

The Power of Our Values
"We won't compromise what makes us special."

Customers and markets are interested in much more than your product, service, or offering. They want to see who *you* are. What makes you different from others? What do you believe?

Most teams have a statement of values listed on the website. You know what's even better? A story! Tell us about a time your values drove your decision making. These are "how" stories, and they bring your identity and deepest convictions to life in unforgettable ways.

Find your story!

Tell me about a time when you (or we) powerfully lived our values, even though it may have come with a cost.

What happened?

Front

Example of *The Power of Our Values*
"Anyone Can Save a Life"

It's not too often that someone in Medical Billing, like me, gets to save a child's life. But that's what happened!

On my social media, I saw a story about a little girl in Venezuela who was suffering from a medical condition that happens to be a speciality of the researchers here at our hospital. And I thought, "that kid looks like a good match!" Of course, I'm no doctor. So I decided to just call Dr. Wilbur, who runs the research in this area. I was nervous about calling someone as senior as Dr. Wilbur but he was completely attentive! He said the case sounded interesting, but we would need to know more.

So I went back to social media and got in touch with this family and I said "I might have a possibility for you."

Soon, we had the entire family on a flight to Houston. We even raised money for their airfare! Today their little girl has completed treatment and is healthy and happy.

Here, we have a value of "people first." And that's real. It doesn't matter what your role is in the organization. Everyone here is responsible for "people first."

Back

Continuity
● Novelty
Transition

Imagine If We Had That Here
"A possibility with power."

A story is a great way to bring a vision to life. The only problem is that the vision is in the future. How do you tell a story about something has hasn't happened yet?

One great way is to reach outside of the organization and bring in a possibility that exists elsewhere.

Sometimes this external story can come from a world that is wildly different from yours, which can powerfully engage our team to make the translation: "our context is very different... But what would that look like if we had that here?"

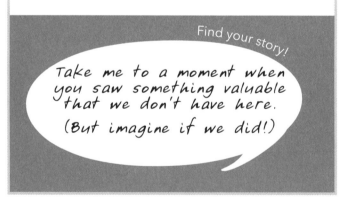

Find your story!

Take me to a moment when you saw something valuable that we don't have here.

(But imagine if we did!)

Front

Example of *imagine If We Had That Here*

"Print Your Own Shoes"

When I was in New York last week, I had some time to walk around Manhattan after meetings. I went into this really cool shop that sells custom athletic shoes.

And I mean these shoes are *completely* customizable! You can choose features on a computer kiosk, and even upload your own artwork to go on the shoes. There's an amazing "shoe printer" that produces your shoes right there while you wait! I was blown away. The process was just so engaging, and I came home with exactly the shoes that I wanted. I'm *invested* in these shoes!

We are in an age where technology has made mass customization possible. *What if we had that?*

In our industry of consumer medical devices, we never talk about that kind of customization. But why not? Think about how varied our customers' needs are. What do you think it would look like if we brought some level of choice to our customers, and then engaged them *emotionally* in the process? What do you think our version of the "custom shoe printer" would look like?

StorytellingLeader.com

Back

Continuity
● Novelty
Transition

Us at Our Best
"Imagine if more people did that!"

Sometimes the possibility for change comes from within your organization or team.

Whenever a person or a team demonstrates exemplary behavior, you have a golden opportunity. Elevate that behavior! Make sure everyone can see it!

As the body of theory called Appreciative Inquiry shows, these stories of "us at our best" are powerful attractors that draw people forward. The more you tell these stories, the more you'll see the desired behaviors start to emerge within the system.

Find your story!

Tell me about a time when we were at our best as we acted on our mission, and it made you feel proud.
What happened?

Front

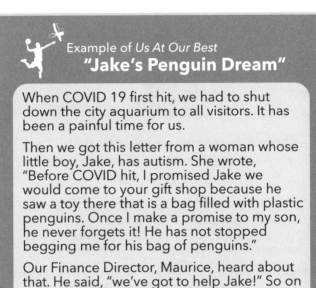

Example of *Us At Our Best*
"Jake's Penguin Dream"

When COVID 19 first hit, we had to shut down the city aquarium to all visitors. It has been a painful time for us.

Then we got this letter from a woman whose little boy, Jake, has autism. She wrote, "Before COVID hit, I promised Jake we would come to your gift shop because he saw a toy there that is a bag filled with plastic penguins. Once I make a promise to my son, he never forgets it! He has not stopped begging me for his bag of penguins."

Our Finance Director, Maurice, heard about that. He said, "we've got to help Jake!" So on Saturday, Maurice drove to Jake's house an hour away. He presented Jake with the toy penguins as a gift from the aquarium, and he said he saw Jake come alive.

Then he also presented Jake and his mom a special invitation to come to the aquarium later this week, where Jake will get to help our keepers feed the penguins!

Running this place is complex, and we all work hard. But imagine if we all reconnected with that kind of joy and dedication every day. Just think how unstoppable we would be!

Back

Continuity

Novelty

• Transition

One Courageous Personal Step
"We can overcome barriers with behaviors."

We think of organizational change in terms of grand strategies. But the reality is that change happens when people make decisions to do something different.

Here's a pro tip: What behaviors do you wish you would see more of on the team? *Tell stories that have those behaviors in them.* Stories work like simulators: The listener "experiences" them in a way that creates a sort of muscle memory – as if the listener had actually exercised that behavior. These stories are a powerful path to organizational change!

Find your story!

Tell me about a moment when you saw someone (maybe yourself) make a step toward our desired change. What did they do? What happened?

Front

Example of *One Courageous Personal Step*

"Transparency Is Listening"

We've been talking for more than a year about building our culture of customer transparency. To be honest, our progress has been slow. This is a hard journey!

That's why I'm so impressed by what Sanjay did on Monday. He called Rohan, the COO over at BioGyzer, and said "I'd like to set up a second meeting with you."

Rohan said, "It's no use, Sanjay. We've already decided we're not hiring your team. We're going with your competitor."

Sanjay said, "I know. I'm not trying to change your mind. I just want to come sit and listen, because I don't think we listened to you very well during the RFP process."

So Sanjay drove over, and he spent the afternoon just asking Rohan questions. He didn't try to sell anything. He just listened.

At the end of the meeting, Rohan said, "I'm really touched by this. This is the kind of partnership we value at BioGyzer." Now Rohan is actively looking for projects for us!

I'm so inspired by what Sanjay did. Imagine if we all listened with that kind of humility. I bet it would make our customer transparency culture come to life.

StorytellingLeader.com

Back

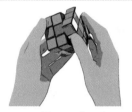

Continuity

Novelty

● Transition

Eureka!
"What it looks like when we solve tough problems."

These "process" stories are powerful, and leaders miss the opportunity to tell them all the time.

Let your stakeholders see what it looks like when you or your team are solving tough problems with creativity and ingenuity.

These stories are especially compelling when you structure them like a mystery: "We tried something, and that didn't work... And then we tried something *else*... And then finally we found the solution."

Find your story!

When was a time that you or the team had to solve a tough problem? How did you finally get to the solution?

Front

Example of *Eureka*
"Counting Phone Poles"

We were serving a $3 billion utility company and we needed to monitor the location of every electrical transformer in the region.

This was nearly impossible because in this rural part of the world that data just didn't exist. We were amazed that no one had it!

The idea of driving around to find every utility pole was a nightmare, like needles in a country-sized haystack. We were stumped.

I remember the team was working late right here in this conference room and eating pizza when Anja, one of our junior team members, said, "You know what? I bet we could create an inventory of all of those utility poles using a basic web browser, Google Street View, and an artificial intelligence engine to analyze the images, and identify and count the poles."

I nearly dropped my pizza! What a brilliantly simple solution! So Anja created the code, and now we offer this software to other municipalities around the world. It's a great piece of software... but we always say that innovation is more than cool software. Innovation is team members like Anja who think differently to solve big problems.

StorytellingLeader.com

Back

Appendix 2:
FREQUENTLY ASKED QUESTIONS

Here are the questions that people ask most often after they have spent some time working with their stories.

Q: Are there cultural differences to how we exercise this? How does this change if I work with a company in a different country?

A: I work with a lot of multinational companies, in which American leaders must engage their Asian audiences, German leaders must engage their Indian audiences, and so on. Yes, there are some differences, but what is most significant are the similarities.

All human beings tell stories. Story structure is the same in every culture. I've had leaders across the United States, Europe, Asia, and Africa construct their stories on the Story Canvas with equal success. No adjustments are necessary.

One of the biggest differences is in the expression of emotion. I remember one leader in Amsterdam confessed that he thought my expression of emotion was "a bit big," and others have found some of my video examples "*so* American." That is, the emotions seem a little syrupy, or the music is overly dramatic. One person told me, "Americans want everything to be like Disney." (By the way, these conversations may sound harshly critical, but they aren't. I invite them. Talking about cultural differences can be really engaging.)

Conversely, I've recommended to those same leaders that when they present to their colleagues in New York, they are welcome to loosen up their reserved style and risk a little more intimacy.

All of this is just a matter of "adjusting the dial" of emotion. Adjust it up or down as you think is appropriate to suit your audience.

But still tell the story. I've heard stories from leaders in South Africa, India, the Philippines, Russia, South Korea, and beyond. I promise you, the language is universal. In the most beautiful way, the stories are the same.

Q: Do all stories have to follow the sequence in the Story Canvas? Do my stories have to include all of those elements?

A: Stories do not have to always follow the Story Canvas. The structure on the canvas is *archetypal* (universally true). It will always serve you well. For the purposes of learning and building your skill, it's a great place to start, so I recommend following the Canvas as you find your confidence.

But stories are extremely malleable. Quite a few of my stories in *Story Dash* do not adhere exactly to the Canvas. Remember the story about Tom, who struggled with the Ken Robinson presentation? There were several Canvas elements missing from that story. For example, there was no "time and place marker," and there was no "until finally."

The story about Dharya the programmer in Chapter 1 was even more sparse. One might argue that it barely qualifies as a story! That's okay. It served my purposes without having to build out every single item on the Canvas.

Using even a few elements of the Story Canvas can make your message more engaging. The more you employ all of the Canvas elements, the stronger the connection you can create.

You can also play with sequence. For example, it's possible to start with the end or the middle of a story … and then zip back in time to tell the beginning: "So how did we find ourselves in this crazy situation? Let me take you back to how all of this started …"

Again, get comfortable executing the structure on the Story Canvas. And then start to experiment and play.

Q: How long should my story be? (Can I speed my story up?)

A: This question usually comes up after we've developed and told multiple stories in the Story Dash. The process tends to produce a series of fully developed stories. After hearing several of these similarly structured stories in a row sometimes people say, "Can't we make some of these stories shorter?"

You can. And you should.

It's true—if you tell several complete "so there I was" stories in a row that all track directly to the Canvas, your audience may start to notice something is going on.

So break 'em up! In conversational speech, the vast majority of our stories are fragments. This has been the case with several of the stories I've told in this book. (Again, the Dharya story is an example of this.)

This is where the "5-30-90" technique may serve you well.

That is, after you have developed the full version of your story on the Story Canvas, be prepared to tell a 5-second version of your story, a 30-second version, and also a full 90- (or more) second version.

For example, I told a very long story across Chapter 5 about my research around the 30 percent hypothesis. The long version was appropriate for a book manuscript. But if I was in fast-moving conversation, I might choose to tell my 5-second version:

"You know, I have this hypothesis that 30 percent of your communication as a leader should be storytelling. In fact, I even verified that once by analyzing speeches like TED talks!"[1]

There's a good chance that this 5-second story will intrigue my audience and someone will say, "Wait a minute. What? 30 percent? TED talks? What do you mean? Tell me about that!" Now we're in an ideal scenario where my

---

1 Okay, so I timed it and this one comes out to around 7 seconds. Let's not get legalistic.

audience is actively asking for me to tell them more. We love that. (Especially when we are in a sales conversation). With that invitation I now get to tell my 30-second or 90-second version: "Okay, so what happened was, I went to the TED website because I had this theory I wanted to test…"

But even if the audience doesn't ask, that's okay. At least I got to drop the key data points into the conversation:

- I've done an analysis of effective communications.
- I've concluded 30 percent of your communication should be story-telling.

It was important to me for you to hear those messages and my 5-second narrative was a great way to work them into the conversation.

Be ready to tell the 5-, 30-, and 90-second versions of each one of your stories. Then read your audience and be ready to adapt in the moment.

Q: When you tell me a story, aren't you just manipulating me?

A: I am telling you stories in *Story Dash* because I believe in this work, I am excited about it, and I am convinced about its potential to transform your work, your voice of leadership, and perhaps even your conception of yourself. I want you to believe it, too. I want you to feel it and get excited about it, and then try it.

Is that manipulation? I call that "conviction."

I might point out that the word "manipulate" is value neutral. It simply means "to move." When I go to my chiropractor, I want her to manipulate my spine so that I leave more aligned than I was when I went in.

As a leader, you are tasked with creating movement and alignment too—either within your team or across your markets. If you believe in what you are doing and you are bringing value and equity to your system, then telling stories about it is not only a noble pursuit, it is at the very heart of your responsibility as a leader.

Q: Once I find a good story, I feel kind of weird telling it over and over again. Is that normal?

A: I feel that way too. The idea of a "narrative asset" is that the story is so valuable, and the results it generates are so dependable, that you will find yourself telling it over and over again. To some, this might feel awkward.

When I speak to a group, if I see someone in the audience who has heard my material before, I feel a little self-conscious that they are going to hear some of my stories a second time. I want to bring spontaneity to the groups I work with, and to have someone say "I've already heard this" feels a little embarrassing. I've asked other trainers and speakers about this, and they confess to feeling the same way.

I think it's just part of the territory of being a leader of influence. I don't have a solution that eliminates this dynamic, but there are ways to mitigate it. When I have multiple engagements with the same organization, I'll make notes of which material I used with which groups so that I bring as few redundant messages as possible.

Ultimately, though, I am more committed to the message and the outcome than to avoiding repetition. When I believe in the story, that is stronger than my vain desire to be perceived as wholly original and spontaneous in every interaction.

In the epilogue, I describe how my friend Becca has told her "Dorris at the beach" story multiple times. I will never get tired of hearing it, and for the sake of the mission I hope she never stops telling it.

Q: Isn't there a dark side to storytelling?

A: This question almost always comes up, because everyone has seen how populations of people can be powerfully swayed by toxic narratives. Dysfunctional relationships, abusive cult behavior, and fascist abuses of political power are all-too-common examples of phenomena that are enabled by stories. Yes, storytelling can be dark and even deadly.

I'm lucky to work with my brilliant colleague Michael McRay, whom I have mentioned earlier. He has written a book about this very topic, called *I Am Not Your Enemy: Stories to Transform a Divided World*. He writes, "I believe some of the highest goals of storytelling, of crafting narratives about our lives, should be cultivating empathy and telling the truth in service of reconciling relationships. Stories are powerful, muscular devices. Storytelling can transform us, whether toward better or worse versions of ourselves. The stories we tell and the ones we listen to change us all the time, in large and little ways, and we'd do well to consider carefully which stories win our attention."[2]

Be mindful that you wield a great power as a storytelling leader. Our charge as leaders of integrity is to tell stories that move people and systems toward equity and wholeness.

Q: Does the story have to be true?

A: One of my favorite questions! The short answer is "yes." Your stories should be true. As leaders, we are in the business of representing *what is* and *what could be.* When you tell stories that misrepresent the truth and you get called out on it, the cost to your credibility and influence is high. It isn't worth it.

But then there's "the long answer," in which I might respond, "What do you mean by *true?*" I have a friend who is a priest, who says, "The question isn't whether our sacred text is true. The question is, *in what way* is it true?"

The Greek concept of "mythos and logos" acknowledges that truth can be either representational or literal. For example, if I told you the old fable of the tortoise and the hare, including its lesson that "slow and steady wins the race," and I asked you, "Is that true?" You would likely say, "Yes, that's true." In other words, you recognize that the representational language says something truthful and helpful. That's mythos. However, you would *not*

---

2 Michael McRay, *I Am Not Your Enemy: Stories to Transform a Divided World* (Harrisonburg, VA: Herald Press, 2020).

assume that the story was *literally* true ("logos"). We don't think that there really was a race where a determined tortoise actually beat a complacent rabbit.

We often switch comfortably between mythos and logos, even in organizations. Many organizations have their own mythology, including founding stories that have morphed over the years so much that nobody can say "what actually happened" all those years ago. Those "mythic" stories still hold values that are vital to the identity of the system.

As a leader, the key is to be transparent so that people aren't mistaking your representational truth for literal truth, or vice versa.

Q: What do you do when the organizational culture is full of negative/toxic stories?

A: Your organization has a shadow side. Human systems always contain dysfunction because they are made up of imperfect people. To be a storytelling leader is to allow space for the shadow stories to be heard. Your job is not to shut them down. Rather, it is to bring them into the light, acknowledge them, and then say "yes, *and* ..." and then invite the stories of *us at our best*: "Yeah I know, things are a mess around here. I've seen it too. We have a lot of work to do. *And*, here's what it looks like when we are exercising amazing resilience and creativity." This gives people a vision to move toward. The best response to a bad story is a better story.

In *Appreciative Inquiry*, which is a story-driven approach to organizational development, Dr. David Cooperrider writes of the "heliotropic principle" of organizational change. In botany, heliotropic plants such as sunflowers turn their faces toward the sun. Likewise, organizational systems are heliotropic in that they tend to grow toward the positive images and stories that are continually placed in front of them.

As a leader, you have more power than you know. A great way to show up in your shadow-filled culture is to start amplifying the credible "us at our best" stories.

Q: Is (X) the same thing as a story? (Is an elevator speech a story? Is a brand a story? Is my pitch deck a story? And so on.) Can you help us with those things?

A: If we go with the classic definition of a story as I'm using it in *Story Dash*, then no—none of those things are technically stories.

This is a bit of a contentious topic. Story theorists can go way down the rabbit hole on the question "What is a story?" My friend Paul Smith is a brilliant consultant on the topic of stories in leadership, and I appreciate his definition when he says simply, "Stories are about *people* and the things that happen to them." Agreed.

Thus, an "elevator speech" is not a story. Defining a clear, thirty-second articulation of your value proposition *is* a valuable exercise, and I'm a proponent of knowing your elevator speech. But it's not accurate to call it a story.

These days, business people are using the word "story" to describe a lot of things that aren't stories. In fact, when I get calls from leaders who say "I want you to come help us with our story," my first line of inquiry is to find out what they mean by that. Frequently they are referring to the "message logic" or "overall structure" of their presentation or pitch deck. Similarly, many people are referring to "brand message" as a story.

One helpful distinction is between narrative and story. Your presentation deck or brand message can have "narrative elements"; that is, it can begin with a problem and have an arc where it lands with a satisfying resolution (even if you haven't named a protagonist or time and place).

When someone calls me and says, "We need to work on our story" and "story" is singular, that's my clue that we need some clarity. You don't have "a story." You have multiple "stories." My work is to step out with you into the always-flowing stream of stories that define your reality, scoop our hands down into that flow, and see what good things we can find.

And yes, we can then bring those powerful narrative assets to create engagement around your pitch deck, your brand message, and more.

Q: How did you get into this work, David?

A: I actually tell one of my vocational "origin" stories in the Leadership Story Deck. (You can find it on Card #13: "The Leap: My old skills bring new value.") I started my career as an advertising copywriter, working for big advertising agencies in Dallas, Texas, and Atlanta, Georgia, in the 1990s. I got tired of writing about hamburgers all day every day, and so I left the agency world because I wanted to write about leadership and teams and innovation. I still bring my old advertising copywriter sensibilities to my work in organizational leadership.

My "blue pill" moment of immersion into the Matrix of organizational storytelling happened in the late 1990s when I was doing some work for The Coca-Cola Company in Atlanta. They asked me to create a communication solution to help employees understand what a "learning organization" was. (See my comments about *organizational learning theory* in the next Answer section.) So I wrote a crazy fable about a flock of sheep that outwits a pack of hungry wolves, displaying the capabilities of a learning organization in the process. I had my illustrator friend Bobby Gombert create some funny drawings of wolves and sheep, and I titled the crazy story *Outlearning the Wolves*.

It was fun and weird and honestly when I first presented it to my client I thought there was a decent chance that Coca-Cola would never hire me again.

Later a publisher picked up the book, and it ended up being translated into more than a dozen languages and selling more than a quarter million copies around the world. I started hearing stories of corporate groups that were mounting stage productions of *Outlearning the Wolves*, and even one police precinct in Japan that presented a *Wolves* puppet show as a catalyst for change. The *Wolves* phenomenon caught me off guard and made me ask myself, *Why did this approach work so well in so many cultures? What was the mechanism by which it created so much engagement, and also led people into a learning dialogue?* That inquiry put me on the story path. It turned out to be so much fun that I stuck with it.

Over the years as I experimented with the topic and worked with leaders to find and tell their stories, the learning offering called The Storytelling Leader evolved. It has been a wonderful journey that has taken me around the world where I've had the honor of hearing amazing leaders tell unforgettable stories. What a crazy ride it has been.

Q: What are your theoretical underpinnings?

A: My approach to organizational narrative (and much of my worldview) is heavily influenced by:

Appreciative Inquiry: This approach to organizational development draws on positive stories as a source of human potential and energy that can propel the system toward change.

Organizational Learning Theory/Systems Thinking: When I was in my twenties and doing learning work with The Coca-Cola Company, Peter Senge's *The Fifth Discipline* was seminal in my engagement with the organizational world. Systems theory, with its acknowledgment of purpose-driven design, multi-causality, and counterintuitive levers for change, was a mindblower to me as a young dude. And Chris Argyris's Ladder of Inference construct invited me into a conversation around knowledge construction and sense making—activities which are always happening when we tell stories.

Complexity Theory: Conversations around complex adaptive systems, emergence, and self-organization link to conversations of story. All systems have an "attractor" around which organization occurs. If I drop a handful of marbles in a bowl, they will all bounce around and eventually organize around a point at the bottom of the bowl. That's a simple attractor, and in social systems the attractors are seldom so intuitive. In complex social systems, the stories we tell are often the most powerful attractors around which people organize. Legendary author and mythologist Joseph Campbell believed that "If you want to change the world, you have to change the metaphor."

Social Constructivism is Lev Vygotsky's theory of knowledge that says our world and everything we know is created by human beings as a product of our language. When we speak, we are creating. People usually think of stories as delivering some value or outcome that comes later, but an intervention is happening *in the moment of telling*. Cooperrider calls this the *principle of simultaneity*, but I love how science fiction writer Ursula Le Guin said it even more simply: "Words are events."

In terms of story thinkers, my intellectual mentors (some of whom are now good friends) have included Joseph Campbell, Stephen Denning, Annette Simmons, Paul Costello, David Boje, Robert McKee, Cynthia Kurtz, and David Snowden.

Appendix 3: HOW to FACILITATE a STORY DASH: NOTES for LEARNING LEADERS

A Story Dash is a facilitated process. With *Story Dash*, I am inviting team leaders and facilitators everywhere to activate stories and the "voice of leadership" with their teams.

Your results will be best if you have two basic skill sets:

- Facilitation skills for team learning
- Comfort with the content of *Story Dash*—at the very least by having read the book and gone through the process individually

If possible, the team learning process is greatly helped if participants have also read *Story Dash* in advance. If that's not possible, the role of the facilitator is increased. It will become more important for the facilitator to provide insight and context for each part of the process.

Note that Certification Training is available if you wish to more fully equip your learning, innovation, and design facilitators to deliver a Story Dash (or the full "Storytelling Leader" program) to your organization.

Materials you will need

- A copy of the book *Story Dash* for every participant so that each participant has access to the six Story Dash Cards in Appendix 1. Each participant should have their own set of these cards. Or, alternatively, a copy of the Leadership Story Deck for every participant.
- One large printout of the Story Canvas for each participant. Ideally, the Canvas should be printed on "tabloid"-sized 11 × 17–inch card stock (in the United States) or A3 paper (in Europe and Asia). You may download a copy of the Story Canvas at www.StorytellingLeader.com. (Note that the Story Canvas is available for your use under a Creative Commons license BY-SA 4.0. You may review the details of this license at https://creativecommons.org/licenses/by-sa/4.0.)
- Copies of "Make Your Story Better," which are also available at www.StorytellingLeader.com.
- Plenty of yellow Post-it "sticky" notes. The classic, square size works best. In the United States, the dimensions are 3 × 3 inches (8 × 8 centimeters).
- Pens
- Snacks and coffee

Setting up the workspace

The Story Dash process is dynamic and active. There is a lot of movement and a variety of interactions that take place in full group, small group, and individual contexts. Some activities require a tabletop space for writing and working, while others require pushing away from the table so participants can face one another in a small circle.

Thus, for a Story Dash, it's best to have a flexible space that is easily reconfigured. If your organization has a training room or a modern innovation/design space where chairs and whiteboard partitions can be easily moved around, that is ideal.

That said, I have seen the process work in a cramped conference room with a long boardroom-style table. This process can work within your space limitations.

The ideal setup is:

- A large room with an open area where chairs can be placed in a large circle, with no tables between them.
- Another area of the room where people can move to tables or desks so they can work with their cards and Story Canvases.
- Space for privacy and confidentiality. Note that sensitive content frequently emerges in story conversations.
- The space should be large enough that multiple teams of four can space out from one another and have conversations without distracting other groups. Having individual "breakout" rooms or spaces for each team of four works well.
- To invite a spirit of reflection and openness, a setting away from the office works beautifully. A retreat-like setting or cool offsite space with good energy can help the process.
- If you choose to use the video that is the "Introduction to the Story Canvas," you will need a projector and sound system.
- A facilitator table for your materials and supplies.
- Access to snacks and coffee; and a catered lunch, if you wish. (The entire program will take around four hours.)

If "ideal" is not possible, at the very minimum you will need:

- The ability to move the chairs. (Avoid auditorium rooms with stadium-style seating or university lecture-style rooms where tables and chairs are bolted to the floor.)

- Enough space to push chairs away from the conference table into the margins of the room so participants can face one another.
- Facilities for multiple groups of four to be able to work independently from one another.
- Privacy; a door that shuts for confidential conversations.

Purpose and audience

Who are you bringing together for the Story Dash, and toward what purpose do you want them to tell stories? Recall that in Chapter 1 there is a section called "Who is this book for?" It details some common reasons why teams might want to engage in a Story Dash. That language may be helpful as you clarify your purpose.

The Story Dash works best with an intact team that has shared responsibilities. That way, they can collaborate while finding and crafting their stories for an outcome that they hold in common.

However, I frequently conduct the Story Dash process with "individual contributors" from separate functions or companies who bring different challenges. The Story Dash works just as well in this cross-functional scenario and does not require modification. (However, participants may find themselves explaining their unique challenges and scenarios in more detail to create shared understanding.)

If you are bringing a team together for a specific challenge or outcome, be sure to articulate that purpose to the team.

Welcome, and "why story?" (10 minutes)

- Create a shared awareness around the reason we are spending this time focusing on story by asking: "Why do you think we are we focusing on storytelling today? Why is story important for the work that you do?" Solicit multiple responses. You won't have any trouble generating a conversation here! People will say things like:

—It's emotional.

—It's memorable ("sticky")/it's engaging.

—It allows you to create a picture so you can *see* what the leader is talking about.

—It's more relatable/more human.

—It makes complicated topics easier to understand.

—Everyone does it/it's universal.

- Affirm the great responses. If you wish, you may borrow language or ideas from Chapter 1 of *Story Dash* to further make the case for why storytelling is important.

- Make the connection that we want to bring all of those powerful ideas into the urgent work that *you* (the participants) are doing *right now*. You will leave with stories that are ready for you to tell so you can advance your work.

- If there is a specific objective for this Story Dash, make that connection here. ("For our response to the new client's RFP, we want to show up differently than we have in the past; we want to show up with this engaging and memorable *story* language that you just described. We want the client to believe in the creative power of this team," and so on.)

Story Mining *(30 minutes)*

Review Chapter 2 of this book, "Story Mining," to familiarize yourself with the intent and approach of Story Mining.

- Introduce the purpose of Story Mining: "Story work is *strategic*. We want to tell the right stories, so we will focus first on *selection*."

- Introduce the cards. These will either be the six Story Dash Cards, which you can procure at www.StorytellingLeader.com, or the full deck that is the Leadership Story Deck, which you can explore or purchase online at Amazon or at www.StorytellingLeader.com. (If you wish, you may use both sets of cards during the Story Dash process.)

- Review how the cards are structured, with the story type and description on the front and the story example on the back. Explain the power of reviewing the example, as described in Chapter 2: If you find yourself stuck and not able to think of a story, read the example. It is more likely to trigger a story by making you go, *Oh yeah, that reminds me of a time when ...*

- If, as the facilitator, you already know the challenge about which you want your team(s) to tell stories, you may wish to narrow down the cards in advance (perhaps by using the black selection cards in the Story Deck): For example, "Go ahead and draw cards numbered 3, 7, 13, and 18 now and review those first. This is just to get you started. But you may find that other cards in the Deck trigger a better story idea ..."

- Walk through the cards you preselected. Describe them, and why you think they might be relevant to the challenge at hand.

- Clarify that the outcome of Story Mining is only to generate multiple ideas. Think of an example of a story and write down a title. "Our purpose is *not* to try to tell the story at this point. We will focus on construction later."

- Clarify that the intent is to go for quantity. "Get as many ideas as you can."

- Clarify that participants will work individually.

- Distribute sticky notes.

- Allow seven to ten minutes for participants to work individually.

- Debrief everyone's experiences. "How did that go?"

- Have participants select a *single* story from their Story Mining exercise that they would like to develop in the next step of the process. (Later they can go back and work on some of the others.)

Story Canvas *(1 hour)*

- Introduce the idea that we want to tell this story for *impact*. (If you wish, you may discuss "neural coupling" as described in Chapter 3. "These boxes on the Story Canvas are the elements that, when you trust them and place them in your story, create a powerful moment of human connection.")

- Present the Story Canvas so that participants will understand the elements and what makes them powerful. You have several options for bringing them into the content:

  1. Find your own language, based on your reading of Chapter 3, or your own expertise about the theory of narrative construction.
  2. Read them excerpts directly from Chapter 3.
  3. Play the approximately ten-minute video, "An Introduction to the Story Canvas," which can be found at www.Storytelling Leader.com.

- Distribute sticky notes.
- Allow a full thirty minutes for each team member to work individually and develop their story on the Story Canvas.
- **If you are comfortable making the offer,** tell participants that they may call on you for coaching if they get stuck. Expect some participants to struggle with this process. (That's okay! The learning is in the struggle.)
- Debrief everyone's experiences. "How did that go? What was it like exercising this way of thinking?"
- Note that this may be a good place to take a break. Tell them to be prepared to tell their stories when they come back!

Breathing life via the "Tell Test"
OPTIONAL initial step:
"Story Theater" *(45 minutes)*

This step is not described specifically in Chapter 4. But it is always a part of my process when I work with groups. (However, it doesn't work with a small team of, say, four or five members.)

- Invite a "brave volunteer" who would like to step forward and tell their story first to the full group.
- Have that volunteer step up in front of the room. I encourage them *not* to bring their Story Canvas with them. Having the Canvas in this setting is actually a distraction, and the teller will be tempted to "read" the Canvas. (If the teller is anxious or feels strongly that they want to keep the Canvas nearby in case their memory goes blank, I will relent.)
- Applaud the first volunteer when they step up, which creates audience energy and highlights the significance of the telling.
- Applaud and thank the volunteer when they finish as well. A story is a gift. "Great job! Thank you!"
- **If you are comfortable,** provide some coaching and feedback, as described in Chapter 4: "Breathing Life via the Tell Test." (If you are not yet confident in your coaching capability, focus on appreciative feedback for now: "Here's what you did that really worked for me …")
- Invite *appreciative* feedback from the audience. "What worked for you? What did you like?"
- Remind them that we are warming the team up, because soon they will be responsible for coaching one another in their small circles. "Our intent is to build this as a shared, team capability."
- I repeat this cycle a total of three times: Volunteer tells; I provide coaching; group provides appreciative feedback. Doing this three times with three tellers will take around forty-five minutes.

The Tell Test in groups *(60 minutes)*

The intent of this exercise is to make sure that *everyone* has an opportunity to tell their story; and also that *everyone* has an opportunity to provide their feedback and coaching to at least two other stories that they hear.

The ideal group size for a story circle is four people, although three and five are okay. It is possible to do this in pairs, but the coaching is more difficult for a team that is new to this process when in pairs. In the event of pairs, focus only on appreciative feedback, and not on coaching for improvement. If there is a group of five, instruct them to be more efficient and mindful of how they manage their time. Avoid groups of six: Six rounds are simply too much content, and participants will become fatigued.

- Review the instructions: "I am about to place you into groups of four (or three or five). Your process is: The first person will tell their story. After they tell their story, provide some appreciation. Then provide your feedback. What worked? What would make it even better?"
- If you did Story Theater as previously described, the three volunteer tellers do *not* need to tell their stories again. Place them in groups of four so each becomes the fifth member. They can still provide feedback to the stories of others, but there's no need to repeat their story.
- Provide the resource "Make Your Story Better." Explain what this resource is: "To support you when you are coaching your team mate on their story, you may wish to consider this resource. It will give you some ideas of the most common areas where your support might provide some leverage."
- Allow the teams a full sixty minutes for this conversation.

OPTIONAL step: "Twice Told Stories"

- If you have quite a few groups (say, five or more), you may wish to introduce a process so that some of the groups can choose one of their stories and bring it before the full group. Part of the power of this is that each group will select one story to "bubble up" and be told a second time to the full group, thereby instituting a filtering process so that the best/most important stories are being identified.
- You can explore a robust process for doing this called "Twice-Told Stories," which has its origins in the work of both Cynthia Kurtz and Paul Costello, and is featured in my book *Circle of the 9 Muses: A Storytelling Field Guide for Innovators and Meaning Makers.*

Where do we go from here?

You have many options!

- Facilitate a conversation on how to keep this work alive in the team. If you are the leader, you can set your expectation for how this will show up in the team culture and identity.

- If you have the luxury of time, have participants select another story to develop. They won't need as much time to build it on the Canvas. (For fun, you can increase pressure by saying, "You have to do it in ten minutes this time! Go!") And then invite them to another round of story circles.

- Brainstorm upcoming opportunities to tell their stories. You may wish to assign "homework": "You must find an opportunity to tell your story to your team/stakeholders/customer. Be prepared to come back to your team in this program and report how it went!"

- In the full-day program that is the Storytelling Leader, I place participants into teams and have them create a "story-driven presentation" around one of their current projects. I show them the "30 percent" information and some sample maps (like my "Do Schools Kill Creativity?" timeline map) to provide a vision for how the stories might show up in their presentation. Then I send them to breakout rooms and give them ninety minutes to come back with a presentation containing a minimum of three stories. This is high pressure!

Teams take turns presenting to a fictional audience (played by me, in the role of a "tough customer").

- If there is an actual-use case ahead of you (for example, "the big client presentation in a couple of weeks"), then be even more mindful about building in multiple iterations of finding, telling, developing … and constantly revising and improving until it feels "right."

Go deeper!

If you're ready to take the next steps in learning and capacity building:

- Invite a custom-designed, professionally facilitated Story Dash process to your team.
- Dive even deeper into building story skills (with applications for culture, knowledge work, strategy activation, branding, and more) with the full-day Storytelling Leader program.
- Certify your facilitators to deploy Story Dashes and ongoing narrative capacity building across your organization. Additional resources and skill building are available for your team of learning practitioners.
- Learn more at www.StorytellingLeader.com.

Appendix 4: HOW I STORY DASHED "STORY DASH"

All throughout *Story Dash*, I've told stories. My intent has been to create engagement and belief by telling stories. I'm not just advocating for a process with a series of steps; I'm inviting you into a way of thinking.

Story is powerful because it is an *invitational* language.

I've spent much of my career in organizational communications, and I can tell you from experience that nearly all leaders' default language is *propositional*: "Here's something I want you to know." Their desire is to faithfully replicate messages into a lot of peoples' heads without any signal loss. If I had taken that approach with this book, I would have simply told you what I want you to think is true, with the hope of replicating that information in your head. Indeed, I could have moved a lot faster by simply making a series of propositional statements:

- "Your clients want you to show up with a more humanized voice."
- "You need to tell stories, and you should feel urgency around this."
- "Stories create a different and powerful kind of connection, and by telling them you could have a transformational effect on the system."

I'll say it again: There are a *lot* of books on organizational storytelling that are written exactly like this, without ever telling any stories. It is bewildering.

The problem with propositional statements is that they invite you, the reader, into a *critical and judging* orientation. (Not *criticizing and judgmental,* which implies an assigning of value.) That is, a series of propositional statements will prompt you to say things like, "Well, that's not true for me at all!" Or maybe "I agree with the author's second point, but I disagree with the third point." As an influencer, this is not the spot I want to be in! I don't want a debate where I am trying to prove my truth to you while you resist.

So instead, I tell stories, which is much more subtly persuasive. Instead of saying *"You* should show up with a humanized voice" (and risk you resisting this confrontational idea), I instead say, "Let me tell you about a group that was losing in the marketplace because they weren't showing up with a humanized voice."

This changes your orientation. When listening to a story, you are no longer *critical* or *judging.* You didn't "disagree" with my story. That language doesn't even make sense. Instead, you simply receive the story … and then have an internal conversation in your own head: *You know, I wonder if there might be some ways our team is like the Boston team that David talked about …* Now *you're* doing the work. Maybe this will spark a flash of insight for you. If it doesn't, that's okay. We'll keep talking. I have more stories.

I'm not telling you what to think. I'm inviting you to engage.

Furthermore, I'm not an illusionist with secrets to keep. I'll show you how I did all of my tricks. Here is how I used stories to lead you into the Story Dash conversation.

I told these stories in Chapter 1:

- Technology team in Boston
- Dharya the programmer
- Elliot's appointment
- Healthcare team wants the training
- Tennessee Prison for Women

I told these stories in Chapter 2:

- Steve Denning/Zambia
- Elizabeth can't think of a story
- How I created the Story Deck
- Nicolas at the beach

I told these stories in Chapter 3:

- Hema's SARS in Bangalore
- Bill separates his software story into two stories

I told these stories in Chapter 4:

- Sherry's failed "customer culture" story
- Jeff Bezos's "clarity of angels" expectations
- Sherry's new and improved Starbucks story

Note that the entire chapter is written in case study language in which I continually point back to Sherry's story; and I also describe my process in narrative language. Although a "rolling case study" may not follow the classic story structure, it relies on many of the same elements.

I told these stories in Chapter 5:

- My story research process (another rolling case study)
- Tom thinks 53 percent is too much
- Story saves the bad presentation in Ohio

I told these stories in the Epilogue:

- "Dorris at the Beach" story
- A "single organism" at the Jonesborough story festival

The six Story Dash Cards feature these example stories:

- "Francisco's Garden" (example of *It Was True at the Beginning*)
- "Anyone can Save a Life" (example of *The Power of Our Values*)
- "Print Your Own Shoes" (example of *Imagine If We Had That Here*)
- "Jake's Penguin Dream" (example of *Us at Our Best*)
- "Transparency Is Listening" (example of *One Courageous Personal Step*)
- "Counting Phone Poles" (example of *Eureka*)

Chapter 1 stories
Technology team in Boston

This was the story on the very first page, where Jeanette introduced me to her technology team who didn't want me there. She said, "If we win, it will be because of people."

Why I told it, in a single sentence:

This story animates a thesis that is central to this book: that leaders are being called to show up in a "more human" way in today's organizational environment, and that storytelling is a path to doing so.

Other objectives:

- To reveal something about myself, my work, and my personality. I'm answering the question that all readers have: "Who is this guy, what has he done, and why should I listen to him?" I want you to feel connected to me as your guide in this book. (Aristotle refers to this as the "ethos" of the speaker.)
- To show that "story" has a place in high-stakes business environments. That quarter-billion-dollar payoff should grab your attention.

Dharya the programmer

This was the brief, not-even-a-complete story about the young programmer in India who said, "It's like, everything I'm doing now is about people."

Why I told it, in a single sentence:
This story answers the question "why story?" by demonstrating the shift in thinking from a technical or transactional "content" focus to the messy "human" focus that all leaders must make.

Other objectives:

• To demonstrate that this work can show up in every culture. (Later in the text I will reference experiences in France, Germany, Asia, and beyond.)

Elliot's appointment

Summarized from Antonio Damasio's book Descartes' Error, *this was the story about the man who had brain damage that separated emotion from thought, making it impossible to make even simple decisions.*

Why I told it, in a single sentence:
This story animates my thesis that "organizations are emotional systems," and also an important mental model: that our emotions lead our decision making and that rational thought "follows."

Other objectives:

• To draw from neuroscience for credibility, and to demonstrate that I'm not just making stuff up. :-)
• To invite you to reflect: What are the "emotional currents" in your organization that you have not recognized or addressed? I'm building a case for urgency for you to tell stories.

- To offer you paths to dive deeper into this topic if you're interested. (Damasio's work is worthy of your attention.)

Healthcare team wants the training

This was the short story about my team that called me back after initially canceling the story program and saying the story work was now "urgent."

Why I told it, in a single sentence:

I am justifying the "dash" part of this book's title, and demonstrating that this process is suited to a hectic, high-stakes environment.

Other objectives:

- To show you a client whose thinking evolved from "I don't think storytelling is that important" to believing that it is an urgent business imperative. The fact that this client was dealing with true "life-and-death" decisions makes their choice to focus on story even more compelling.
- To invite you to a similar "conversion" in seeing the urgency for story work, especially if you are still resisting and are not yet a "believer."
- To show you applications of stories in different industries. I started with a technology application; now you've seen healthcare. (More are coming!)

Tennessee Prison for Women

I made a quick reference to a prison inmate who described storytelling as "a different kind of intelligence."

Why I told it, in a single sentence:

I told this story to provide a testimonial that backs up the claim that some people have a "profound" experience with storytelling.

Other objectives:

- To show yet another contextual application that is very different: This can even be exercised with prison inmates. (And, in fact, the applications of storytelling in social, justice, and equity contexts are incredibly rich.)
- To invite you to reflect on the intriguing idea that story exercises a "different kind of intelligence." Note that I didn't pause to explain what that might mean; I want you to be reflective and curious about it in the same way that I was.
- To reveal the heart of my own values. I want you to see more of what I care about in the world.

Chapter 2 stories
Steve Denning/Zambia

I excerpted the "Zambia" story from Steve Denning's book The Springboard. *This was the story about the healthcare clinic in Zambia. It was a "story about story" that illustrates the impact that Steve had on the World Bank by telling a story.*

Why I told it, in a single sentence:
I told this story to illustrate one of the most important claims of this book, which is that a story can be a catalyst to "unsticking" the system, with the possibility of significant change.

Other objectives:

- To show a new industry application: financial.
- To illustrate another application of story: creating internal alignment around a strategic change. (This one is near to my heart, because it is the focus of a lot of my work.)

Elizabeth can't think of a story

This was a "rolling" story across Chapter 2 that depicted Elizabeth struggling with story work, then trusting the Story Dash process, and ultimately triumphing with a powerful personal story.

Why I told this story, in a single sentence:

This story introduces some of the very real difficulties that people run into when they start working with stories, and positions the Story Dash process (and the Story Dash Cards and Leadership Story Deck) as solutions to overcoming those difficulties.

Other objectives:

- To introduce a reassuring tone in the event that you are feeling similarly anxious about this work: "Don't worry. I am here to help you."
- To show a new culture (France), and a new industry (consumer products).
- To show how even the most worthy of projects (waste reduction) have a hard time manifesting without stories to bring them to life.

How I created the Story Deck

I explained the genesis of the Leadership Story Deck, based on my experience of noticing patterns after hearing thousands of stories.

Why I told this story, in a single sentence:

Because the Story Deck (and Story Dash Cards) are central to the Story Dash process, I want you to appreciate the thoughtful care and testing that went into the design so that you will be more willing to invest your attention in these resources.

Other objectives:

- To more explicitly spell out some of the challenges that storytelling can address (such as knowledge transfer, culture and identity work, and so on).

Nicolas at the beach

This was the story Elizabeth told about her young son who found her company's products polluting the shore at the beach.

Why I told this story, in a single sentence:
I told this to show an example of a story that is both well-told and strategically focused so that you can envision what is possible when one trusts the Story Dash process.

Other objectives:

- To validate the "fear" idea that I introduced earlier, and show how some people experience a feeling of risk in this work; and also to show the payoff when one leans into the risk.
- To demonstrate how "personal" stories like these can have a tremendous impact within the organization.
- To show how story can generate traction around a stuck project. In this way, the Nicolas/waste reduction story is similar to the Denning/Zambia story.

Chapter 3 stories
Hema's SARS in Bangalore

In this story, a leader who participated in the Story Dash process brought a vulnerable story to a team of "intimidating" leaders, which resulted in systemic movement.

Why I told this story, in a single sentence:

I told this story to demonstrate that trusting the Story Canvas structure can create visceral moments of human connection ("neural coupling") that compel people to action.

Other objectives:

- To illustrate the change that can happen in a room ("something shifted") when leaders tell stories.
- To show how a well-constructed story can transcend poor or average speaking skills. ("It's not about performance.")
- To suggest something about the role of *courage* in this work.
- To illustrate "leading up," showing how story is a potent lever for managing those who are higher in the organization … and also for building your own influence.

Bill separates his software story into two stories

This short illustration shows how Bill overcame the confusion of his software story by splitting it into two stories.

Why I told this story, in a single sentence:

I have made the point that having multiple conflicts in a story may be an indicator that the story should be split into multiple stories, and here I am giving a practical illustration of what that might look like.

Chapter 4 stories
Sherry's failed "customer culture" story

This story depicted a leader who, after telling her "Starbucks story," was disappointed in the outcome.

Why I told this story, in a single sentence:

I told this story to illustrate that "we aren't done yet" with the process:

Simply relying on the cards and Story Canvas won't guarantee a good outcome; you need to "breathe life" into the story by telling it to someone.

Other objectives:

- To establish a "before and after" story that will provide an overall narrative arc for the chapter.
- To invite you to action by explicitly asking you how you would coach Sherry's story. This is a skill-building activity.
- To show a new application for story: culture and team identity work (and also organizational learning).

Jeff Bezos's "clarity of angels" expectations

Jeff Bezos has institutionalized the story capability for senior leaders at Amazon, and he has set high demands on his leaders to practice it.

Why I told this story, in a single sentence:

I told this story to validate again that a leader of influence has made a significant investment in building story capability, proving it is a skill that demands intention and organizational investment.

Other objectives:

- To show how "deep" this capability can go, with the idea that it may take "a week or more" to develop a story at Amazon … and to invite you to imagine making a similar commitment to building this skill.
- To build my case by drawing from an influential organization that has made an investment in storytelling ("Wow, if the richest guy in the world is focusing on this …").
- To show the discipline this work requires. This work can be hard!

Sherry's new and improved Starbucks story

Sherry responded to coaching and came back with a much better version of her "Starbucks" story.

Why I told this story, in a single sentence:

I told this story to show a good outcome of intentional coaching … while also giving you an opportunity to imagine how you might show up in this support/coach role.

Other objective:

- To give you a vision for the effort that may be required to develop your narrative assets. Sometimes it comes easy, but most of the time you gotta work it!

Chapter 5 stories
My story research process (rolling case study)

This was a long rolling story in which I introduced the fear of "overdoing this stuff," and how I studied TED talks to test the "30 percent" hypothesis.

Why I told this story, in a single sentence:

I told this story to give you a vision for how you might position your stories in your "real world" applications, and to show how they might be balanced with other forms of rhetorical persuasion.

Other objectives:

- By positioning much of this chapter as a "Eureka" story (as described in the Story Dash Cards), I'm engaging you in my process and conclusions. The 30-percent balance is one of the critical "strategic awarenesses" I've identified for this chapter, and so I'm embedding it in a story so it will stick. I'm practicing what I am preaching.

- To return to the "fear" concept that I introduced at the beginning of the book, because I know this is when many leaders start to experience doubts. I want to give you confidence that "you can do this!"

Tom thinks 53 percent is too much

Tom responded to the Ken Robinson TED talk with his misgivings about my "53 percent story" conclusion.

Why I told this story, in a single sentence:
Anticipating the doubts that some readers may be having at this point, I am giving voice to them by having Tom speak those misgivings out loud.

Other objective:

- To avoid spending too much time in "didactic/telling." More than previous chapters, this chapter is dense with data, graphs, and theories. Following my intuition that I was placing demands on my audience's fatigued brains, I once again took an opportunity to practice the principles I'm advocating in this chapter. I am breaking up the didactic "telling" with a story.

Story saves the bad presentation in Ohio

I observed a presenter delivering a "bad" strategy presentation … which he finally "rescued" by telling a story.

Why I told this story, in a single sentence:
This story introduces a new idea—my "dimmer switch" model of attentional energy—and gives this concept a spotlight with a story to bring it to life.

Other objectives:

- Again, I am practicing the methods I'm advocating for in this chapter, by having just two or three "big ideas" in the chapter and embedding those big ideas into stories.

- To invite you to reflect on the heuristic that "two minutes of story buys nine minutes of attention" so that you might exercise it in your own work.

Epilogue
"Dorris at the beach" story

This is the story that Becca Stevens, founder of Thistle Farms, tells about taking Dorris to the beach for the first time.

Why I told this story, in a single sentence:

I am making the case that stories link to something deeply human, and have the potential to awaken us to the most sacred parts of ourselves.

Other objectives:

- It's a an especially beautiful, well-crafted, and meaningful story. I want you to see another example of "good."
- I am committed to the work of Thistle Farms and will take every opportunity to engage people in the mission. I am proud to end *Story Dash* with an invitation for you to support this worthy work. Here's the website again, in case you missed it. :-) www.ThistleFarms.org

A "single organism" at the story festival

This was my description of the International Storytelling Festival at Jonesborough, TN, and my observation that a crowd experiencing a story together is a "single organism."

Why I told this story, in a single sentence:

I'm still making the case that something special and rich is happening when we engage with stories, and suggesting that it has the ability to unite us in a powerful way.

Other objectives:

- I am setting up the idea that follows, that some deeper desires (for hope, transformation, and transcendence) are drawing people to story.
- I live in Tennessee, and it would be a crime for me to not give a shoutout to the International Storytelling Festival, and my friends in Jonesborough!

Acknowledgments

Thank you, friends and colleagues who looked at early versions of the manuscript and provided thoughtful feedback: Mary Alice Arthur, CJ Casciotta, Sherry Deutschman, Emory Hutchens, Robbie Hutchens, Jim Karrh, Matt Keyser, Janet McDonald, Michael McRay, David Nour, Clint Padgett, Dick Richardson, Becca Stevens, Ricardo Troiano, and Jim Woods.

Thistle Farms

Serving on the board of Thistle Farms has been one of the great joys of my career. Thank you, Becca, for stories that call people to something beautiful and true, and for the reminder that the best stories are not the ones that we tell but the ones that we courageously live. Thank you to the rest of my beloved friends and partners at Thistle Farms, including Hal Cato, Shelia Holli Anglin, Simpkins McClain, and the entire team of survivor leaders.

You can join the story at www.ThistleFarms.org.

CEDEP

Deep appreciation and forever gratitude to my friends at CEDEP, a special community of learners just down the road from the fabulous Palace of Fontainebleau in storybook Fontainebleau, France. For more than seven years now, I've been a visiting professor at Le Centre Européen d'Education Permanente. This cozy campus by the Forest of Fontainebleau has been my home for experimentation.

Dean of programs Jens Meyer once said to me, "You can try anything you want here. You are safe. You cannot fail." I took him up on that offer. Almost everything you read in *Story Dash* has been tested there, along with more than a few ideas that didn't work. Thank you, CEDEP family: Frank Azimont, Loïc Sadoulet, Jens Meyer, Thomas Hinterseer, Wim Wuyts, Christophe Gillet, Philippe Colongo, and the whole amazing team. I'll meet you in the bar for a Moët & Chandon.

Learn more at www.CEDEP.fr.

Experience to Lead

Thank you to my partners in leadership development at Experience to Lead, where you will experience the coolest leadership learning available. Join us to hear stories from Olympic and Paralympic athletes at the Olympic Training Center; or astronauts and scientists at NASA's Johnson Space Center; or hit songwriters and producers and performers in Nashville. Story + Immersion + Your Challenges = Leadership Transformation. Thank you, Dick Richardson, for twenty-five years of friendship and mentoring.

Learn more at www.ExperienceToLead.com

The Matt Holt and BenBella team

It was May 2020. COVID had just hit a couple months earlier, all of my clients had canceled all of my work, and I was still reeling from the collapse. I remember sitting on the back porch with my wife, Robbie, watching the sun go down, and I said, "I'm stuck. I can't see what's next."

A little while later, I got an email from a guy named Matt Holt who said, "I think you have another book in you."

Doors don't always open in a magical moment, but when they do you never forget who was there issuing the invitation. Thank you, Matt, for starting this.

Thank you, BenBella team. Sarah Avinger, Leah Wilson, Elizabeth Degenhard, Monica Lowry, Katie Hollister, and Mallory Hyde, you are creative, collaborative, and gracious.

The Hutchens family

Thank you, Robbie. I know I am loved.

Thank you, Emory and Ollie. You are loved.

Rosie, you are a good girl. Yes, you are.

Thank you, Mom and Dad, Jay and Johnny, for your presence while the Hutchens family story is changing.

Index

ABOUT the AUTHOR

A former advertising copywriter, David Hutchens has been working at the intersection of complexity, narrative, and organizational learning for more than twenty years. He lives with his wife, Robbie, in Nashville, Tennessee. He is Emory and Ollie's dad.

www.DavidHutchens.com

www.StorytellingLeader.com

TAKE *your* STORYTELLING CAPABILITY *to the* NEXT LEVEL!

Bring the power of story to your group, team, project, function, or system! There are lots of ways you can engage, and offerings that can support you along your leadership journey.

You'll find what you need at www.StorytellingLeader.com.

Find the value-holding stories about your work that you didn't know you knew! Get the Story Deck as well as other materials to support your team.

Build story capacity across your team and culture with the premier active learning experience! Available as a classroom or virtual program.

A process for finding, developing, and activating the urgent stories you should be telling *now*. Get all the tools and resources you'll need to unleash the team... or invite our facilitators to support you.